RESET YOUR BARCODE

Praise for
Reset YOUR Barcode

"The principles and lessons in *Reset Your Barcode, Five Steps to a Financial Reset* are timely reminders of the steps we all need to take to succeed in an increasingly complicated world. Reynolds teaches us these lessons with a blueprint we can follow for success."

—**Brad Wilson**, Utah House of Representatives, President and CEO of Destination Homes

"After reading Marv's book, *Reset Your Barcode, Five Steps to a Financial Reset*, I will be putting it on my 'must read list' for friends and family. Marv has a great way of narrating the different ways to look at money and will help you reset your understanding and comply with financial principles. It is an amazing read and so easy to understand."

—**Gwen Peterson**, President, Hope for Widows Foundation

"How lucky can you get? The ideas Marv has used to help hundreds of clients and financial advisors achieve economic freedom are now available all in one place. *Reset Your Barcode, Five Steps to a Financial Reset* is a must-read for anyone interested in financial success!"

—**V. Stan Benfell**, Chairman Beacon Financial, Inc., former President, Security Life of Denver

"*Reset Your Barcode, Five Steps to a Financial Reset* is a fantastic read. Start living the principles and implementing the practices today, and tomorrow you'll be glad you did!"

—**Robert B. Beckstead**, former President Sales and Marketing Association of Utah, and former Vice President of Sage Analytics, consultant to the California Board of Education

RESET
YOUR
BARCODE

Five Steps to a Financial RESET!

MARVIN REYNOLDS

NEW YORK

RESET YOUR BARCODE
Five Steps to a Financial RESET

Published in New York, New York, by Morgan James Publishing. Morgan James and The Entrepreneurial Publisher are trademarks of Morgan James, LLC. www.MorganJamesPublishing.com

The Morgan James Speakers Group can bring authors to your live event. For more information or to book an event visit The Morgan James Speakers Group at www.TheMorganJamesSpeakersGroup.com.

BitLit

FOR ALL THE BOOKS YOU OWN

FREE eBook edition for your
existing eReader with purchase

_____

PRINT NAME ABOVE

For more information,
instructions, restrictions, and
to register your copy, go to
www.bitlit.ca/readers/register
or use your QR Reader to scan
the barcode:

ISBN 978-1-61448-778-4 paperback
Library of Congress Control Number:
2013941513

Cover Design by:
Brett Peterson

Interior Design by:
Bonnie Bushman
bonnie@caboodlegraphics.com

In an effort to support local communities, raise awareness and funds, Morgan James Publishing donates a percentage of all book sales for the life of each book to Habitat for Humanity Peninsula and Greater Williamsburg.

Get involved today, visit
www.MorganJamesBuilds.com.

Habitat
for Humanity®
Peninsula and
Greater Williamsburg
Building Partner

This book is dedicated to the cause of freedom and all those who are willing to accept the responsibility that it requires.

Economic freedom is the foundation to *all* freedoms.

CONTENTS

ACKNOWLEDGEMENTS

No one ever succeeds alone. Nowhere is this statement truer than it is with me. This book could not be possible if it were not for the help and support of countless people. Though I could never name them all, I would like to make special mention of a few.

Special thanks to my wife Julie for putting up with me all these years. Without her unique gifts to our relationship, I would only be half a person. Thanks to my business partner, Brett Peterson. His ideas and faith in me—along with freeing up the necessary time to undertake such a project—is worth more than he could possibly know. Thanks to Kalie Chamberlain for her skill in formatting and editing this work. Thanks to Morgan James Publishing for having faith in me and giving their support to getting this book published.

And special thanks to my family, friends, and clients for their support and encouragement in this and the many other activities I could not have pursued without their help.

INTRODUCTION

Part I: Reset Your Barcode and Reset Your Life

What does it mean to reset your barcode? First, let's talk about the barcode, and then we will talk about what it means to reset it and why it is so important.

A barcode, otherwise known as the Universal Product Code (UPC), appears on most products. When scanned, it reveals the assigned value of the product. This allows for a very efficient checkout process and inventory management system.

Whether we know it or not, we are like these products—we each have an invisible barcode on our person. When we come in contact with other people, we quickly scan them and assign a perceived value. We also keep track of an inventory of desired qualities, or value, we expect from other people. When we perform our scan, if we like the value revealed, we pursue a further relationship with that individual. If we perceive that the value we are looking for isn't there, we usually pass on the relationship, at least for now.

Why Assign a Person Value?

Of course, assigning a value to another person is a very difficult and dangerous thing to do. Nevertheless, we do it. Because we want to be successful and happy, we instinctively know that for this to happen, we must surround ourselves with successful and happy people. In other words, achieving success requires the help and cooperation of others. Cooperation demands that each participant in the cooperative be able to make a contribution of some kind. Just like the Little Red Hen, we don't like to share the fruits of our labor with someone who won't contribute to the effort required to enjoy success.

Since making a valuable contribution to any cooperative effort is so vital, it helps to know where real contribution comes from. All contributions are based on a person's **character** and **competence**. These two elements are the foundation upon which all contributions are built. **Character** is what a person believes and what they do based on those beliefs, and **competence** represents their skill and wise use of knowledge.

When character and competence add up to represent the contribution you are looking for, you usually assign a pretty high value to that individual and proceed to develop a cooperative relationship with them. Naturally, when those elements are not present in sufficient quantity, the relationship is not pursued, and the offer to cooperate is not extended.

Reading a Barcode Accurately

Reading the barcode and assigning the proper value is difficult and takes a great deal of practice. Sometimes, people are so unsure of the value they provide that they will try to divert your attention away from character and competence by moving their barcode from an obvious and useful location and place it where they want you to focus your attention. For example, some will try to place it on an object such as a luxury automobile or a big fancy house, brand name clothing, or even different parts of their anatomy. All this is meant to keep the focus on superficial things rather than expose their deficiency of high-quality character and well-developed competence. Don't get me wrong. I'm okay with nice cars and homes and clothing. That's beside the point. What we really want when we scan each other is an accurate reading of the quality— the character and competence that can substantially contribute to a cooperative effort leading to success and happiness.

So why is it so important to reset your barcode? Because when you are scanning others, they are scanning you. As you look for character and competence in them, they are looking for it in you.

Why Should I Reset My Barcode?

Because you can't change anyone else, **you must concentrate on changing you**. What is it about your character and competence that creates a high-value reading sufficient to make you an attractive contributor to their cooperative? What values drive your performance and make you valuable to them? If you are not continuously making improvements in your character and competence, which will affect the reading on your barcode, you will substantially limit your opportunities for success.

Part II: Values, Principles, and Virtues

From the day we are born, we begin experiencing life. We learn from watching others; we learn from personal experience; we learn from observing nature and our environment; we learn from friends and teachers. Much of what we learn is good and useful. Some of what we learn is harmful and limiting. Because what we learn has a powerful impact on the values we choose, and because our values eventually shape our character, it is critical to do a self-assessment from time to time to see if our values are helping or hurting us.

Once our values are established, they become our automatic responses. Automatic responses are what make up our **presets**. And, of course, we all have them. Our presets can have some benefits in that they allow us to do many things on autopilot; in other words, we can act without giving much thought to what we are doing. However, sometimes this can be very detrimental because when we operate on autopilot without thinking, we may be holding ourselves in a flight pattern that will fly us into the ground. Being slightly off course can leave us miles away from our destination.

Presets are great if they are helping us get where we want to go, but too often, this is not the case. The evidence for this is overwhelming. All we have to do is watch the news, and it becomes painfully obvious that not all presets are healthy.

Understanding that our presets are in large measure responsible for the value reading that shows up when our barcode is scanned makes it important—no, *essential*—to evaluate and periodically reset our presets so we can get past the things that hold us back and move forward to create a high value reading of character and competence when our barcode is scanned. Resetting our barcode is something that we can and should do over and over as we strive to reach our full potential and the ability to make our maximum contribution.

Doing a reset of any kind must begin with an understanding of values, principles, and virtues and how they affect every aspect of our lives.

Values—Our Personal Preferences

It's absolutely critical to understand that **values are actually nothing more than personal preferences**. For some, this statement is a little difficult to swallow at first because their values represent who they are.

Once we choose our values, they become important to us. In fact, if we value them enough, they begin to take on a sacred nature. If you don't believe me, just try telling someone that their values are wrong; then, brace yourself for a battle. Most of us will fight like a wildcat to justify and preserve our values.

The problem here is that **values can be good and bad**. Just because we value something does not make it right or wrong, good or bad. For example, throughout time, there have been those who held the value that freedom was only for the privileged few. Most people today, at least in this country, believe that *all* men were given certain unalienable rights, such as freedom to pursue life, liberty, and happiness.

Principles—Laws of Nature

It's a good idea to periodically compare our values to principles. **Principles are natural laws**, the kind you don't get to vote on. They are universal, timeless, and changeless; they have consequences and they are impartial. In other words, principles just *are*. They don't care if you value them or not. You simply comply with them and receive a positive consequence or violate them and receive a negative one.

You can tell when a concept or practice is based on a principle or not by simply observing how it plays out over time. If a concept is truly principle-based, it will always lead to order. Order is what you get when you have peace, harmony, beauty, cooperation, and success over the long term. When you are not dealing with a principle-based concept or practice, you will always end up with chaos. That's what you get when you continually have to intervene and do patch work to make something work out.

What If a Principle Is False?

Supporting and following a false principle is what I call building on the beach while the tide is out. At the moment, it may look like a good idea. There may be plenty of property close to the water in the short term; however, when the tide comes back in, you end up underwater and are likely to get washed away.

I like to give ideas, concepts, and practices what I call a "stress test" to see how well they hold up in good weather and bad, or when the tide is in as well as out.

Lots of professions use a "stress test." Physicians apply the "stress test" by connecting a patient to various monitors and then putting that person on a treadmill to see how he/she responds to exertion. Engineers place substantial weight on a structure to see how much it can bear. And financial institutions are supposed to check their financial strength to see how much loss they could sustain and still be able stay in business.

In every case, they are looking to see how much stress can be borne before weakness, chaos, and disaster appear. When they reach the right level of durability, the product receives approval because it will be able to perform its proper function for the long haul.

Many concepts and practices in our modern society will not pass the "stress test." They have been tried over and over again throughout history and have repeatedly ended in disaster. That is because they are not principle-based. When concepts are principle-based, they always lead to order. That's why it is important to periodically stress test our values to see whether or not we are building on the beach while the tide is out. If so, we may want to adjust our values to be sure that they are compliant with correct principles so we don't end up under water.

Virtues—the Foundation of Character

Now let's contrast values and principles with virtues. You see, virtues are what you end up with when you learn to value correct principles and practice them until they become part of your character. **Virtues are character strengths or positive character attributes**.

When your character is made up of values that are built upon a foundation of correct principles, you will possess strength of character, or virtue.

Part III: Reset Your Barcode and Gain Financial Freedom

So what does that have to do with finances? Well, today it seems the whole world is experiencing what we have called a financial crisis. That would indicate that many of our financial concepts and practices are not holding up under stress and are therefore not resting on the foundation of principles. In other words, we have lost our financial virtue. My contention is that the financial crisis is symptomatic of a much bigger problem, one I call a *character crisis*.

If we are going to fix our financial problems, we will first have to fix our character problems. The only way this will be possible is to stop using the concepts and practices that caused the problems in the first place. We must restore financial virtue. In order to do that, we must rediscover the financial principles that will stand the test of time, bring back order, and restore virtue. This means we will have to begin with ourselves. We must examine our financial values, compare them to financial principles, and make changes where necessary to comply with the principles and strengthen our individual character. By doing so, we can restore personal and financial virtue.

Why Do We Need a Financial Reset?

1. Economic freedom is the foundation for social, political, and religious freedom. If we lose our economic freedom, we lose everything.
2. People who do not plan their future finances are not likely to be able to finance their future plans.
3. Good planning and financial discipline make it possible to enjoy financial freedom and take advantage of opportunities. Remember, luck is what you get when preparation and opportunity come together.
4. People who understand financial principles and follow them enjoy greater quality and simplicity in their life.
5. When we let our finances get out of control, our lives get out of control. Runaway finances become a very demanding and unyielding taskmaster and cause a great amount of stress and unhappiness.
6. Stress and worry over financial problems will stifle creativity and personal growth.
7. Chaos resulting from financial mismanagement replaces order, and life becomes filled with quantity, clutter, and complexity.
8. The way we have been handling our national and global finances is not working. When national finances are mismanaged, it sets a poor example for the nation's citizens and puts an extreme burden on their personal finances through higher taxes and fewer benefits.

Listed above are eight good reasons for us to do a financial reset. But the most important reason of all is that **the value of our contribution goes down dramatically when out-of-control finances govern our lives**. Success cannot be achieved without cooperation. Cooperation cannot be achieved without contribution. Contribution comes from character and competence. The development of character and competence is delayed and minimized when our freedom is compromised by poor financial management. If we do not reset our financial barcode right away, we may lose the freedom and opportunity to do so. That should be all the reason we need.

How Do We Do a Financial Reset?

There are five steps involved in performing a financial reset. Each step has been given an iconic reference so we can easily connect with and understand the importance and meaning of that step.

Here are the steps in order:

1. "The Glass Slipper Experience"
2. "The Ebenezer Experience"
3. "The Wooden Puppet Experience"
4. "The G.P.S. Experience"
5. "The Johnny Appleseed Experience"

As you proceed through the training in this book, you will come to understand and be able to perform each step. These steps will help you prepare and execute your own financial plan, the results of which will be empowering and satisfying.

As you complete the five steps to resetting your financial barcode, you may want to have a notebook handy where you can record your answers to the activity questions that appear throughout the book. You also may want a file where you can store the plans and records you'll create as you complete the steps. So, let's get started.

FINANCIAL PRINCIPLES

In this section, you'll learn how to complete the first step in resetting your financial barcode, Step 1—"The Glass Slipper Experience." This step is so essential because it will build a foundation of financial virtue.

This step is governed by fourteen financial principles that, when practiced, will lead to order and restore financial strength. As we review these principles, let's be sure to compare our financial values to the principles and see if we are setting ourselves up for a positive or negative consequence, for financial order or chaos. When we find an area where improvement is needed, let's have the courage and character to make the change.

The 14 financial principles are:

1. Wealth cannot be created or destroyed. It already exists.
2. Giving generates wealth.
3. There are only 100 pennies in a dollar.
4. There are only two economies.
5. There is only one financial problem.
6. There are only two solutions to that one financial problem.
7. There are only two ways to generate income.
8. Investing does not make you an investor.
9. You cannot spend your way to prosperity.
10. You cannot treat all dollars the same.

11. Money doesn't change people. It exposes their values.
12. Money doesn't buy happiness. It buys options.
13. Money is subject to the "Law of the Harvest."
14. Hoping is not planning.

THE FIRST STEP, OR "THE GLASS SLIPPER EXPERIENCE"

Why a glass slipper? Think back to when you learned the story of Cinderella. What is significant about her story?

On the surface, it would appear that her story is about a fairy godmother, a pumpkin coach, glass slippers, and all the other trimmings that magically appeared to make her a princess. But that's not it at all. The real story is about the girl. It is a story about adversity, challenge, and struggle. It's a story about kindness, persistence, and faith. It's a story about taking the circumstances you've been given and making the most out of them. It's about rising up and becoming your best self.

Consider the fact that Cinderella's mother and father died while she was very young. She was raised by a wicked and manipulative stepmother. She had two spoiled and jealous stepsisters. And she was despised and treated as a servant in her own home.

In spite of years of mistreatment and abuse, she chose to remain kind, gentle, and loving. The more her stepmother and stepsisters tried to break her down, the stronger she became. She refused to let others determine who or what she was. In fact, she did not become a beautiful princess because of the fairy godmother; instead, the fairy godmother appeared because she had become a beautiful princess by virtue of her persistence and kindness and goodness.

The glass slipper is symbolic of what happens when you pursue a course of virtue. You become the "perfect fit" for the thing you are trying to obtain. Consequently, you will attract into your life all the trimmings that will show the world who and what you really are.

Like Cinderella, each one of us is in the process of becoming. Every minute of every day, we are becoming more or less honest, more or less kind, more or less patient, and more or less compliant with correct principles. As we do so, we are choosing for ourselves a future with more or less positive or negative consequences.

Financially speaking, when our lives become filled with principle-based character, or virtue, we become the perfect fit for a happily ever after. When we take short cuts, or violate principles, we will always end up being an ugly stepsister instead.

The key to a perfect fit is to learn the principles and align our values with them. This is how virtue is developed.

CHAPTER ONE

Principle #1:

WEALTH CANNOT BE CREATED OR DESTROYED. IT ALREADY EXISTS.

When you think about wealth and how it works, you soon discover that it is very similar to energy—it cannot be created or destroyed. Rather, it is constantly changing form and changing hands. Wealth is something that already exists in one form or another and has been accessed or harnessed by one person or another. We all know that we cannot take wealth with us when we die, so it is always left behind in some form to someone. Think of the farmer who trades his labor for money. He then trades his money for some land and seeds. He sows the seeds and they become produce. He sells the produce and buys a cow. He sells milk that he gets from the cow and receives money, which he uses to buy more land and seeds so he can produce more crops and sell them for more money. You get the point. Wealth is always changing form and always changing hands.

So why is it so important to understand this principle? There are many reasons, but one of the most important is that there are many who promote the false concept that wealth is a zero sum game. They want you to believe that there is only so much to go around. They teach that if someone else has it, you will have to go without unless you take it from them. Under the guise of equality, they preach that wealth should be redistributed so that everyone has the same amount. These people are either ignorant or part of something far more sinister. Either they don't understand the governing laws of wealth or they are trying to deceive and control you. Don't listen to them. A power plant doesn't have energy; it generates it. The same is true of you. You don't have wealth—you generate it!

Using Wealth for Good

If we want to be wealthy, we must learn the principles that govern wealth. We must learn to access, harness, and use it for good. What goes around comes around. When we use wealth for good, it ends up coming back to us in many forms and in many ways and ultimately creates more wealth for everyone. The worst thing we can do with wealth is to hoard it. It only fulfills its potential when it is kept in circulation.

Consider the following. I have heard that luck is what you get when preparation and opportunity come together. That being said, I believe that **wealth is what you get when a good idea and proper resources come together**.

A great idea is one that solves problems, meets a need, or fulfills a desire. Resources are all around us, but until someone comes up with a great idea on how to use the resources to solve problems, they just lie dormant. However, when the idea and resources come together, they generate wealth.

Take the concept of the railroad, for instance. The railroad is made up of ore that was mined and refined into steel. The steel was made into rails that were laid upon the backs of timber to support the heavy steel. Metal was also used to build powerful engines and boxcars to haul precious commodities from one end of this country to the other. The railroad was one great idea after another, turning raw resources into usable products that solved problems and met needs and desires. It's impossible to measure how much wealth has been generated by the ideas and resources that created the railroad.

Another wealth-generating union involves what I call a second-generation idea and resources. In this case, the money is already there. It is just looking for a problem to solve or a need to meet. At the same time, someone else has a great idea and is looking for the money needed to put the idea into action and bring their combined problem-solving ability to life.

When a young preacher named Frank W. Gunsaulus preached a sermon entitled "What I Would Do If I Had a Million Dollars," little did he know that a wealthy gentleman by the name of Phillip D. Armour was present in the congregation and very interested in the preacher's message. When Mr. Armour's money and Mr. Gunsaulus' idea came together, the Armour Institute of Technology was created. Because of a great idea and the necessary resources coming together, many lives were enriched. This second-generation idea and resources allowed access to a great deal of wealth.

How Does This Apply to You?

So how does this apply to you? When you think of wealth, don't simply wish you had it. Think of a **problem that needs to be solved**, a **need that could be met**, or a **desire that could be fulfilled**. When you consider a problem to solve, be sure that it is one you feel passionate about, something you could put your heart, mind, and strength into. Then, use your imagination and create a way to make it happen. Envision the resources that would be necessary to implement the idea. Consider every possible detail, and begin working to make it happen. Remember, luck is what you get when preparation and opportunity come together. Well, opportunity is everywhere; we just need to do the preparation so we can recognize it and know what to do with it. When we do, our idea and the needed resources will also come together. We will generate wealth and use it for its intended purpose, which is to solve problems, meet needs and desires, and enrich lives in the process.

Remember, wealth is like energy; it cannot be created or destroyed. It already exists. Just as the power plant converts energy from one form to another, you have the ability to convert resources into wealth. This is how we access wealth. The answers to the questions in Activity 1 will likely take some time to find, but if you are really passionate about your idea, it will be worth the effort and may be the source of great wealth to you and others.

When you help others succeed, you succeed with them.

Activity 1
How Can I Use Wealth for Good?

This activity contains several questions to help you discover how to use your wealth for good. Answer the questions to see how you could access wealth.

1. What problem, unmet need, or desire do you feel passionate about?
2. How would you solve that problem or meet that need?
3. What resources would be necessary to implement your idea and bring it to life?

CHAPTER TWO

Principle #2:

GIVING GENERATES WEALTH.

"What goes around comes around." In other words, the things we do will always come back to reward us or to haunt us, depending on whether they're good or bad. Having seen this many times and in many ways, it makes sense to me to try to do as much good as possible. Whether we are giving our time, money, or talents, we receive a satisfying feeling that we are part of the solution because we are participating in an effort to make things better. That good feeling makes us happy. When we are happy, we tend to be healthier. Healthy people tend to be more productive. Productive people tend to be more prosperous. And prosperous people have even more to give. The giver and the receiver experience a benefit spiritually, psychologically, physically, and financially. That's a lot of benefits for just one act of giving.

When we give, we generate wealth. You see, when the giver lifts the receiver up from dependence to self-reliance, the receiver becomes a contributor. As a contributor, the former receiver is now in a position to pay his own way and to become a giver. For every receiver who becomes a giver, you increase the ability to lift two more receivers up from dependence to self-reliance. This is true because instead of one giver and one receiver, you now have two givers. Now that you have two givers, you can reach two receivers. When those two receivers are lifted from dependence to self-reliance, you now have four givers. As you can see, with that process at work, it would only take thirty successful rotations to lift over one billion people out of poverty and turn them into self-reliant givers. Check out the numbers on page 11.

When we give, the cost of dependence goes down, and the reward of self-reliance goes up. Self-reliant people work and earn money and then spend and save it, which helps create jobs. More jobs create more pay. More pay creates more tax revenue and so on. Everybody prospers when every possible person is contributing.

Engage in Personal Charitable Giving

Charitable giving is the responsibility of the individual. Each person should have the right and responsibility to decide for himself or herself how much they want to give and where they want to give it. When that responsibility is assumed by the government, it takes away those rights and responsibilities.

Students understand this concept very well. Just watch what happens when professors take high scores from "A" students and give them to "F" students in order to create equal grades for everyone. The "F" students will be pleased because they no longer have to worry about passing the class, or even studying for that matter. The "A" students, however, will

When Receivers Become Givers

$$1 + 1 = 2$$
$$2 + 2 = 4$$
$$4 + 4 = 8$$
$$8 + 8 = 16$$
$$16 + 16 = 32$$
$$32 + 32 = 64$$
$$64 + 64 = 128$$
$$128 + 128 = 256$$
$$256 + 256 = 512$$
$$512 + 512 = 1,024$$
$$1,024 + 1,024 = 2,048$$
$$2,048 + 2,048 = 4,096$$
$$4,096 + 4,096 = 8,192$$
$$8,192 + 8,192 = 16,384$$
$$16,384 + 16,384 = 32,768$$
$$32,768 + 32,768 = 65,536$$
$$65,536 + 65,536 = 131,072$$
$$131,072 + 131,072 = 262,144$$
$$262,144 + 262,144 = 524,288$$
$$524,288 + 524,288 = 1,048,576$$
$$1,048,576 + 1,048,576 = 2,097,152$$
$$2,097,152 + 2,097,152 = 4,194,304$$
$$4,194,304 + 4,194,304 = 8,388,608$$
$$8,388,608 + 8,388,608 = 16,777,216$$
$$16,777,216 + 16,777,216 = 33,554,432$$
$$33,554,432 + 33,554,432 = 67,108,864$$
$$67,108,864 + 671,08,864 = 134,217,728$$
$$134,217,728 + 134,217,728 = 268,435,456$$
$$268,435,456 + 268,435,456 = 536,870,912$$

$$536,870,912 + 536,870,912 = \mathbf{1,073,741,824 \text{ or } 1.07 \text{ billion}}.$$

protest that they worked hard to have high grades. If their efforts are only going to reward students who haven't earned it, they will simply stop working so hard. Of course, in this situation, everyone suffers as performance and standards are reduced.

Personal charitable giving increases the contribution and cooperation of the giver and the receiver by engaging both in an effort to overcome poverty. In the effort, everyone prospers.

In direct contrast, government welfare promotes and perpetuates poverty by robbing the giver and receiver of incentive and opportunity when it seizes assets by force and distributes them by quota. In this effort, everyone suffers.

If you simply remove a man from the ghetto, he takes the ghetto with him. However, if you remove the ghetto from the man, he is free to go where he wants and leave the ghetto behind.

Why Must I Give My Wealth?

So why is it important to understand and live by this principle? Hopefully it's obvious, but just to be sure that everyone understands, we should not look to government to solve our problems. We should work with each other and retain our individual rights and responsibilities. When we do it, everyone prospers. When the government does it for us, everyone suffers.

"What goes around comes around." The more you give, the more you receive. The more you receive, the more you have to give. Be a giver! Giving generates wealth.

Activity 2

Determine Two Charitable Causes

Write down at least two charities or causes that you are going to give more time and or money to and determine when you will begin.

1. Charity Name.
2. What I Will Give (Time/Money).
3. When I Will Begin.

CHAPTER THREE

Principle #3:

THERE ARE ONLY
100 PENNIES IN A DOLLAR.

W ho doesn't know that? Apparently, a lot of people don't know. Otherwise, we wouldn't have out-of-control spending at the personal and national level. Think about what that simple statement really means. For one thing, it means that one man's pay raise is another man's price hike. If I pay more for labor, I have to charge more for products and services. When a person or group such as a union or other entity demands more pay, unless they have increased productivity and profitability enough to justify the pay increase, they will simply raise the cost of the product/service being produced. That, of course, is because it just became more expensive to provide the needed product or service.

In like manner, if the government thinks it is solving financial problems for those who have not by confiscating wealth from those who have, think again. When you take from the "haves" and give to the "have-nots," you simply raise the cost of goods and services for the "have-nots." You can combat this by placing price controls on the "haves" so that they cannot raise the price for goods and services. But in this case, you simply end up with fewer "haves," which increases the number of "have-nots,"because without the ability to generate profits, you have nothing to pay employees or incentivize investors, which in turn lowers demand for goods and services. The snowball effect of this action also lowers wages and opportunities for employment, so instead of solving the problem, you have done what non-thinking, principle-violating, short-term solutions do, and that is **make the problem worse**.

The only way to justify paying more for labor is to find ways to make labor more productive and profitable. When those two components are in place, you can raise pay without raising prices.

The important thing to remember is that there must be productivity and profitability, and you must account for every penny. Activity 3 will help you evaluate the value you provide your employer.

Activity 3

How Valuable Is Your Labor?

Write your response to the following questions to evaluate how much value you create on the job.

1. What value do you create for your employer?
2. If you were the employer and were making payroll, would you see your services worth what you are paid?
3. What can you do to increase the profitability and productivity of the services you provide?

CHAPTER FOUR

Principle #4:

THERE ARE ONLY
TWO ECONOMIES.

There are only two economies, cash and credit. Let's examine
the difference and see why it is so important to understand this
principle and what we can and should do as a result.

What Is a Credit Economy?

In a credit economy, everything you buy costs more. You see, you borrow
money from the banker in order to buy something from the retailer,
who borrowed from the banker in order to buy it from the wholesaler.
The wholesaler borrowed from the banker in order to buy it from the
manufacturer, who borrowed from the banker to be able to manufacture
their product. In this model, you add layer upon layer of cost to the

price of the thing you are purchasing. When you enter and live in a credit economy, it costs more to live. Your hard-earned dollars only go so far. Why add all that extra expense unless it is absolutely necessary? That alone is a pretty good reason to do your very best to avoid living in a credit economy.

Another reason to avoid a credit economy is because it adds substantial risk of financial failure. Remember in 2008 when Bear Stearns and Lehman Brothers were "sold for a song" or went into bankruptcy because of their extreme leveraging? In other words, they borrowed money using assets as collateral that were only worth a fraction of what they were borrowing. Additionally, the stock market crash in October of 1929 was caused by individuals borrowing money to speculate on stocks. And the most recent crisis in the real estate market was caused by over-leveraging and speculating. As an interesting side note, I think it somewhat bizarre that governments around the world are trying to get us out of the most recent economic malaise by doing exactly what caused it, which is over-leveraging.

Plan for the Inevitable Economic Downturn

The economy inevitably slows down from time to time. You may lose your employment or may be forced to take a reduction in income because everyone around you has either lost their employment or are taking a reduction in pay as well. When this happens, how will you pay your debts? If you can't pay your debts, what happens to your belongings that you have partially paid for? Does the banker grant you a waiver? When the collectors come knocking at your door, do they buy back any equity you may have built up in the asset you owe against? Sorry, it doesn't work that way. You pay or you lose. And when you lose, you don't just lose the asset or belonging; you also lose all the money you have been paying in order to create ownership.

When things slow down in a credit economy and people around you can't make their payments, they are forced to default on their obligations. When they default, the bankers lose money they can't afford to lose. When the bankers lose money, they aren't able to pay depositors their deposits. When that happens, the government has to step in and pay the depositors. Where do you think the government gets the money to pay the depositors? From the depositors, of course—the government gets the money it needs by raising taxes to collect revenue to bail out the failed financial institutions. Seems to me that taking money from someone to pay them back what you owe them is counterproductive. In the end, borrowing to repay debt creates a financial nightmare and substantially increases the risk of financial failure.

Again, this seems like a pretty good reason to avoid credit and debt unless it is absolutely necessary. Having said that, I understand there are times when a person or business has little choice but to borrow some money in order to progress with their financial plans. However, you should never borrow more than absolutely necessary and only if you are in a position to easily afford and quickly pay it back. There is no such thing as "good" debt and "bad" debt—only debt.

There Is a Better Option

The second economy is the cash economy. If you haven't already begun to understand why this is a much better way to live and operate your finances, let me just say that it costs substantially, if not exponentially, less. And the potential dangers and heartache of loss—due to circumstances that may be entirely out of your control—are greatly reduced.

A smart man (my father-in-law) once told me that when it comes to interest, there are two kinds of people, those who understand it, and those who don't. Those who understand interest *earn it*. Those who don't understand interest *pay it*.

When he first taught me this lesson, I didn't fully understand or appreciate it. You see, I needed to buy a car and had saved up about half of the purchase price. Because I valued his input, I took the new car I wanted to buy on a test drive and went straight to his home to have him look it over. Of course, I was feeling pretty good about my selection and the fact that I had half the money I needed to buy it.

His impression of the car and my judgment concerning it was very favorable, which made me feel pretty good about myself, but then the other shoe dropped. He asked me how much the car cost. I told him. Next, he asked how much money I had. I told him. Then, he asked why I was looking at a car that cost more than what I had available to pay for it. My bubble burst. I got the message, took the car back to the dealer, and began shopping for one I could pay cash for. It wasn't what I wanted to do, but I knew he was right. Even though I felt a little disappointed at the time, I became very grateful for his counsel and my decision to follow it. Not having a car payment while I was making a career change reduced my financial pressures and allowed me to use more of my resources to develop my new career.

Understanding Economic Fundamentals

One final word about economics. It's very important to understand the fundamentals that ultimately drive every economy. Simply put, they are inflow and outflow, revenue and expense. I hear economists and radio and television personalities talk about leading and trailing indicators to predict what will happen next in the economy. The problem with using short-term indicators to make predictions without considering the long term fundamentals is you are once again trying to build on the beach while the tide is out. It may make sense in the short term, but in the long term, you will be washed away and end up under water. **The best indicators for long-term financial predictions are inflow and outflow**.

Why? It's simple. Whenever you spend more than you make, or have more outflow than inflow, you are headed for trouble. That is true for individuals, families, businesses, and governments. If you can't raise the revenue you need to cover your expenses, you must lower your expenses. That's all there is to it. When you borrow to cover expenses that you cannot pay for with revenue, all you are doing is raising future expenses. Sometimes you can get away with that process for a while, but ultimately, you will have a day of reckoning, and it is always very painful.

Remember, there are only two economies, cash and credit. Determine today that you will learn to live in a cash economy and enjoy the peace of mind that comes from not having to drag around the ball and chain of debt.

Use Activity 4 to determine whether you are living in a cash or credit economy. Honest reflection will set you on the right path to achieving this financial principle.

Activity 4
Are You Living in a Cash or Credit Economy?
Answering these questions will help you determine whether you are living in a cash or credit economy.
1. How much is your current income?
2. What are your current expenses?
3. Do you have positive cash flow every month?
4. What can you change or do without to reduce your expenses enough to have positive cash flow?
5. Do you have a plan for accelerating your debt elimination so you can live in a cash economy? If not, why not? If so, what is it?

CHAPTER FIVE

Principle #5:

THERE IS ONLY
ONE FINANCIAL PROBLEM.

I t seems kind of crazy to say that there is only one financial problem when there are so many different ways that financial problems manifest themselves, but the truth is still the same: there is only one financial problem. That problem is **you don't have the money you need when you need it**. Think of how true that statement really is. When you don't have the money you need when you need it, you have a financial problem. Otherwise, if you always had the money you needed when you needed it, you wouldn't have a financial problem.

Now that we have established that point, why is it so important to understand this financial principle?

Few of us will ever have enough money to pay for all the things available to spend money on. That being the case, it is important to make sure we know what matters most and to make sure we do what we need to do in order to have money for the things that are most important to us.

We have all heard the statement that money isn't everything, and I agree; however, I still struggle to come up with things that don't require money in order to do them. For example, you might say it doesn't cost money to play at the park. Well, let's think about that for a second. First, how did the park get there, and how is it maintained? Chances are the park was provided and is maintained with tax payer dollars and or public use fees. Somewhere along the way, money is involved. Second, when you go to the park, will you wear shoes and clothing? If so, it is very likely that some money was involved at some point. Third, will you play baseball or basketball or some other sport while there? Again, if you do, you will probably find that money was required somewhere along the way. Fourth, what about a picnic? There is no such thing as a free lunch; nothing is free. I find that in all cases I can think of, everything costs money.

Again, I don't think money is everything, but I do struggle to think of things that do not require it.

Because so many things we do cost someone something, it is imperative that we understand this financial principle. No one likes to have a financial problem. So in order to avoid having one, we need to plan ahead and do what is necessary to make sure we have the money we need when we need it.

Activity 5
How Do I Avoid the Only Financial Problem?
Thinking about how you will finance your future plans will help you avoid the one financial problem.

1. Make a list of the most important things you do that require money.
2. How much money will you need in the future to finance your future plans? These may include retirement, travel, education, etc.
3. What can you do today to make sure you don't end up having the one financial problem?

CHAPTER SIX

Principle #6:

THERE ARE ONLY TWO SOLUTIONS TO THE ONE FINANCIAL PROBLEM.

The fact that there are only two solutions to that one problem is very good news. It keeps life simple. So what are the two solutions? Well, you can grow money so you have it when you need it, or you can buy money so you have it when you need it. This is what I call creating money on demand.

Let's look at these two ways to solve that one problem. First is growing money. What does that mean, and how do you do it?

How to Grow Money

Growing money is pretty much like growing anything else. It takes seeds (or startup money), a "fertile plot" (or a good place to grow), and work—watching over and protecting it. While it is growing, it must constantly be fed and given adequate time. When you try to grow money too fast, you run the risk of harvesting it before it has taken root and grown enough to provide any real value.

Money, like most plants, usually starts out small. But, if you are patient and persistent, continue to feed it, and let it earn interest, one dollar turns into two, two turns into four, four into eight, eight into sixteen, and so on until you have enough money when you need it. Simply put, growing money is increasing your money by gaining interest.

Consider the Rule of 72. The Rule of 72 is a rule of thumb used to predict how long it will take your money to double or compound. It works this way. Divide the rate of return you are receiving on your money into the number 72. The number of times it goes into 72 is the approximate number of years it will take to double your money. For instance, let's say you are receiving a 72% return. In this case, your money would double every year. On the other hand, if it were only earning 1%, it would take 72 years to double. This rule reminds us why we want to get good returns on our investments. But it is also important to remember that it doesn't matter how good the rate of return is if it can all evaporate because it is subject to inappropriate risk.

Another good rule of thumb is if an investment opportunity sounds too good to be true, it probably is. Does the name Bernard Madoff mean anything to you? As you may recall, he was the former chairman of NASDAQ and in 2008 admitted to operating the largest Ponzi scheme in our country's history. Billions of dollars were lost because people invested in something that sounded too good to be true. Many people have learned the hard way that if you take inappropriate risk, you will likely end up with the one financial problem—you won't have the money you need when you need it.

The challenge we face when growing money is that it usually takes considerable time. In fact, for most of us, it takes the better part of a lifetime for our money to grow large enough to cover all of our potential needs. Also, many of our needs must be met while we are still trying to grow our money. This can precipitate a financial emergency. That's why it is also important to buy money.

How to Buy Money

Sometimes people make the mistake of thinking that buying money is borrowing it. **When you borrow money, you are renting**. The interest you pay is the rent for the privilege of using the money. **Buying money is when you use pennies to purchase dollars that show up on demand**. For instance, if your house were to burn down or be damaged by fire, you simply call your homeowners insurance company, and they supply the money you contractually purchased for this kind of event. The same is also true of life insurance. If you die before you've accumulated enough to pay off debt and provide an income replacement to those who depend on you for support, a life insurance company will pay out the face value of your life insurance policy.

Buying money is the second way to create money on demand. This is how you avoid that one financial problem—not having the money you need when you need it. The purpose of all insurance policies is to ensure that you will have money available when it is needed most. Keep in mind that some life insurance policies have cash values that also help you grow money. In summary, if you want to avoid the problem of not having enough money when you really need it, start saving and growing money today, and buy money that will show up when it is needed most.

Activity 6

Planning for Your Financial Future

Answering these questions will start you on the path to planning for your financial future.

1. How much money will it take to provide you with an adequate income when you are no longer willing or able to work?

2. What obligations do you want taken care of if you are not privileged to live long enough to take care of them yourself?

3. How do you plan to meet these obligations?

4. Since there is never enough money available for every possible want, it is important to make a list of the things that are most important to you. These are the things you want to be sure you plan for so you don't get distracted on things that are less important. Make a list of the five most important things you want to be sure you have money for.

CHAPTER SEVEN

Principle #7:

THERE ARE ONLY TWO WAYS TO GENERATE INCOME.

T here are only two ways to generate income—people at work and money at work; these are the only two things you can do to generate the income and the only ways to fund your present and future finances. **People at work** is when you work for yourself or for someone else to generate income. **Money at work** is the result of growing your money until it becomes large enough to generate income from interest, appreciation, and dividends.

Diagram 1—People at Work and Money at Work

Diagram 1. People at work and money at work, the only two ways to generate income.

Let's look at these two ways to generate income. People at work is great because it allows you to make your contribution to others and be paid for it. But it also has its drawbacks if you can't work because you are sick or just getting too old to continue. Thus, it is important to gradually build up money at work so you can stop working and still have income.

So why is it important to understand the principle that there are only two ways to generate income?

1. It is important because you must always be increasing the value you create if you want to keep earning money in a competitive world.
2. It is important to understand if you ever want to stop working and still have income.
3. It is important if you want to fulfill your obligation to those who depend on you, to ensure that the money they need shows up, even if you don't.

If you are like the all-too-typical American, you go to work to earn a paycheck. You use the paycheck to cover your expenses. Since the expenses usually require the entire paycheck, you have to go back to work. This familiar pattern of work → earn → spend is what I call the "Earn and Consume Treadmill." As long as you can keep working and don't overspend the paycheck, everything seems to work out.

Diagram 2—the "Earn and Consume Treadmill"

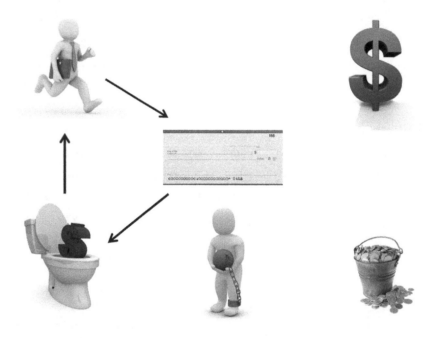

Diagram 2. The "Earn and Consume Treadmill." People go to work to earn a paycheck and then use the paycheck to pay for expenses. When expenses use up all of the paycheck, people have to go back to work.

But sometimes you want more than your current situation will provide. So, like everyone else who doesn't understand this principle, you borrow money so you can enjoy it now and pay for it later. When you do this, you give the controls for setting the speed, incline, and duration on the treadmill over to your creditor. Now the creditor has the power to exercise control over your life. This means you will be running faster, harder, and longer. Again, as long as you can work long enough, this may turn out okay. But if anything at all goes wrong, you will find yourself subject to the demands of your creditor.

Diagram 3—Buy Now, Pay Later

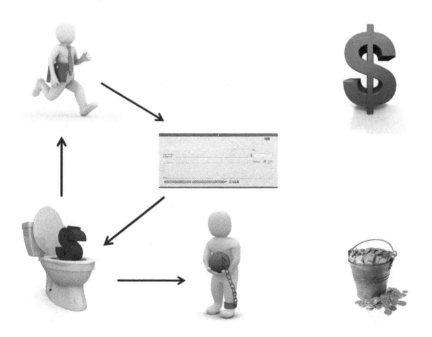

Diagram 3. Buy now and pay later. Essentially, you take on a ball and chain and give the controls for the treadmill over to your creditor. Now, you have voluntarily given up some of your economic freedom.

How Do I Get off of the "Earn and Consume Treadmill"?
So, how do you break this pattern and free yourself so you can get off the treadmill? First of all, you must take control of your spending.

Establish and live by a spending plan that allows you to have surplus cash flow every month. Save your surplus cash flow in an emergency savings account until you have a short-term financial safety net. As you build up your savings, be sure to purchase an appropriate amount of life insurance so that income-generating money can show up when you can't.

Diagram 4—Regaining Financial Control

Diagram 4. Once you get control of spending, you have something to set aside for emergencies and opportunities.

With regular saving happening and life insurance in place, you now can begin to put money in places where it can work for you. As your money works, it generates additional income.

Diagram 5—Putting Your Money to Work

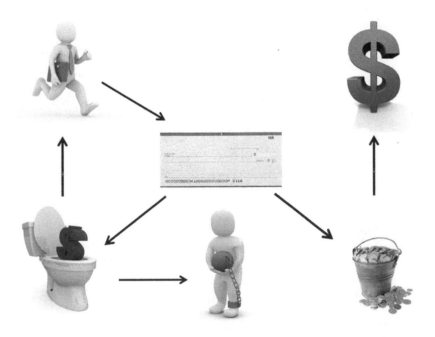

Diagram 5. Here, you take surplus savings and put it to work in appropriate instruments to facilitate growth and tax advantages.

Diagram 6—Money at Work Generates Income

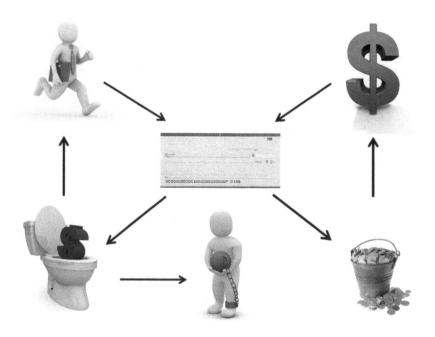

Diagram 6. Money at work generates additional income.

The additional income generated by your money at work can be used to accelerate debt reduction until you are completely debt-free. Once you are debt-free, you can concentrate on growing your long-term income-producing assets. When your long-term assets become large enough to generate an acceptable income, you will be free from the "Earn and Consume Treadmill." Then, you will have money at work and you won't have to.

Diagram 7—Use Additional Money for Debt Reduction

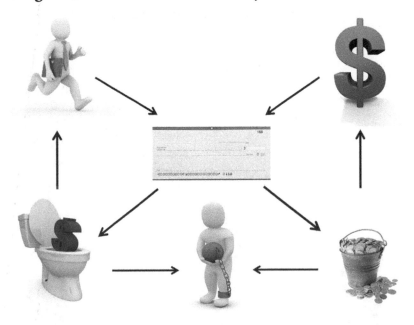

Diagram 7. Take the additional income from money at work and use it to accelerate debt reduction. In time, you will be completely debt-free and be able to focus all of the income from money at work—combined with ongoing savings—to accelerate the growth of your money at work.

If you live by this principle, eventually you will have enough to produce the money you need even when you are not on the "Earn and Consume Treadmill."

Diagram 8—Success, or the Money
You Need When You Need It

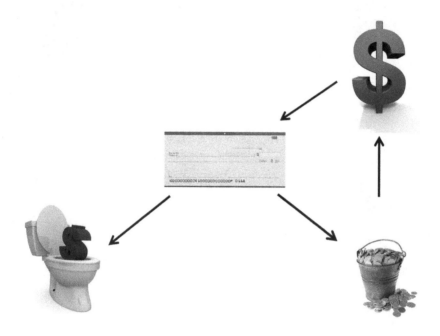

Diagram 8. Financial success. You now have the money you need when you need it, whether you are working or not. That's money at work!

Activity 7
Are You on the Treadmill? Do You Want to Get Off?
Use this activity to determine what diagram best fits your current financial situation.

1. How much are you currently saving each month?
2. Will it provide the benefits you want it to?

CHAPTER EIGHT

Principle #8:

INVESTING DOES NOT MAKE YOU AN INVESTOR.

I n 1974, when the ERISA (Employee Retirement Income Security Act) law was enacted, it was designed to solve problems and prevent abuse by companies who were supposed to fund retirement benefits for retired employees of the company.

You see, up until that time, most retirement plans were defined benefit plans. They paid retirees a defined benefit for the balance of their lives. When ERISA was enacted, it strengthened the requirements placed on companies to reserve enough money to be able to make good on their retirement promises. It also created new sections of the tax code that allowed employers to set up retirement plans called **defined**

contribution plans. Under a defined contribution plan, the employer's responsibility shifts from providing a defined benefit for life to setting aside a defined contribution during your working years.

This change meant the employer was no longer responsible for how the retirement money was managed or how long it lasted the employee during retirement. This removed a huge burden from the employer and placed it on the back of the employee. In many ways, it seemed like a good idea at the time because of perceived potential in the financial and investment markets. Lawmakers assumed that this shift would enable the employees to achieve greater financial results as they selected from a variety of risk-based investment tools that would allow their retirement funds to run faster, jump higher, and stop quicker. Now, the assumption was, we could save less and grow our money faster. Using the Rule of 72 and a false assumption that we could earn an average of 10% per year on our investments, many of us mistakenly thought we could sit back, relax, and expect to have over a million dollars in our retirement accounts by the time we reached age 65.

But Doesn't That Sound Too Good to Be True?

Unfortunately, this law caused some unforeseen and unintended consequences. One such consequence was encouraging people who are not investors to put their retirement money in at-risk instruments. At first, handling their own funds may have seemed like a great opportunity for people who wanted to grow their retirement funds bigger and faster. However, as we have learned, what goes up can and eventually *will* come down. The old axiom that "the market will always go up" may be true, but it might not go up in time for you to recover losses and be able to retire.

Further, with decreased savings and increased spending and consumption by the American people and the government, we gradually shackled ourselves with a massive ball and chain called debt. This process has caused a restructuring of our economy, severely limited market performance, and reduced the likelihood that people's dreams of having sufficient retirement savings will ever happen. It seems that the retirement dream is turning into a retirement nightmare.

What Is a Real Investor?

So what can be done? One of the first things we must do is understand the principle that **investing doesn't make you an investor**. Let's begin by understanding the definition of what a real investor is. In order to be a real investor, you must have the following three things.

1. Risk Capital
2. Specialized Knowledge
3. Influence

Let's examine each in more detail.

Risk capital. A real investor only invests with risk capital. Risk capital is defined as **money you can walk away from both emotionally and financially without damaging your financial stability**. So, if risk capital is "walk away money" or money that you don't need, under what circumstances would money you are going to need for retirement ever qualify as risk capital? Of course, the answer is, it never does. That explains why so many people that are approaching retirement and staring at the prospects of having to continue working because their retirement plans have evaporated. Many now call their 401k a "40notOK."

Specialized knowledge. A real investor has specialized knowledge. Real investors never invest in things they don't know and understand. Their knowledge of how the investment works provides them with the ability to watch for opportunities that give them an advantage— relative to timing and positioning—and then reward them with a worthy return.

Influence. A real investor never invests without having a position of influence. Having the ability to use specialized knowledge and make decisions that influence the outcome are critical to a real investor. When you own 49% or less, you have no influence over decisions that impact the value of your investment.

When you consider the fact that real investors are operating with risk capital, specialized knowledge, and a position of influence, it makes sense that they are able to deal with the two-way street of potential. If it goes well, they may really prosper. If it goes poorly, it's ok, because it was "walk away money" in the first place.

A Lot More Accumulating, a Lot Less Speculating

What percent of the people you know actually have a significant amount of money they can walk away from without really upsetting their financial apple cart? If your experience is anything like mine, the number is very small. Most people aren't saving enough, let alone extra. It should be obvious, based on the level of financial distress that many people are experiencing, that we should be doing a lot more accumulating and a lot less speculating.

So what is accumulating? Accumulating is what an accumulator does. What is an accumulator? Well, it's not an investor. In fact, the defining characteristics of an accumulator are pretty much the opposite of those that define an investor. For example, accumulators cannot afford to lose their money. They don't possess the specialized knowledge to evaluate and make decisions regarding investments. They don't have a position of influence that enables them to direct activities or exercise a degree of control over the outcome of an investment. In short, **accumulators can't afford it**, **don't know what they're doing**, and **couldn't do anything about it anyway**. So, instead of wanting *potential* like the investor, the accumulator wants and needs *guarantees*. Stated another way, an accumulator needs a return of principle and a return on principle. Instead of risk-based instruments, accumulators buy instruments that have guarantees. This is how they influence the outcome. By the way, I believe that **most of us are or should be accumulators**, especially when it comes to our retirement funds.

Don't Gamble with Your Retirement

So what happens when you combine an accumulator with risk-based investments? You create a gambler! Why a gambler? Because that's what gamblers do. Gamblers take money that can't afford to lose, put it in a place where the odds are against them (because they don't understand the risk they are taking), and have no way of influencing the outcome other than luck. When you gamble, it's not about potential or guarantees—it's about luck.

When gamblers are experiencing a losing streak, do they stop and cut their losses? No, they feel they must keep going because their luck is bound to change. When you call your broker after some serious losses on your portfolio and ask if you should get out before it gets worse, what does he say? Doesn't he tell you not to get out now because you will guarantee your losses if you do?

When gamblers are on a winning streak, do they capture their gains and quit while they are ahead? No! Why would you stop when things are going so well? Gamblers keep gambling to make up for all the times they lost money in the past. After a very good run in the market, when your portfolio is up substantially, you call your broker and ask, "Should I get out now and capture my good fortune?" What does he say? Doesn't he tell you to keep going because you are "in it for the long haul"? It all sounds like gambling to me, except for the broker who makes his money whether you are gaining or losing, as long as you leave it with him. Sorry, but it's true.

Where You Put Your Money Is Important

So, before you decide where to put your hard-earned money, ask yourself, is this investor money, accumulator money, or gambler money? If it's **investor money**, you won't need the help of a broker because you know what you're doing and can do it yourself. If it's **accumulator money**, you will need to put it in places where it is backed with guarantees, such as banks, credit unions, and insurance companies. If it is **gambler money**, you can put it in any risk-based instrument you have no control over and see how lucky you are. So, before you ever talk about asset allocation, be sure to talk about asset classification. Putting your money in the right place in the first place is half the battle. **Where you put your money is just as important as the amount of money you have.**

Ask yourself if you would ever take a job like this one. If someone came to you with an offer to be a partner in their company, it might sound pretty tempting, right? Now add the following details. First, you must invest your retirement money into their company. Second, if the company has profits after expenses for the year, they will split the profits with you. However, if there are no profits, then operating expenses will come out of your retirement money. The possibility exists that you could lose your money. And third, you will never have any input into the day-to-day operations of the company. Would you take a job like that? To do so would be putting your money at substantial risk with no way to influence the outcome. Who would take a job like that unless they were dealing with "walk away money"? Most people wouldn't do it even if it were money they could walk away from.

Have you caught the message yet? When you take your money, especially money you will definitely need later on, and invest it into someone else's company where you have no real input into the operations of that company, you are *gambling*.

In addition, when you put your money into mutual funds, you are doing the same thing. Only now, you don't even own a portion of the company stock that you invested in. When you invest in a mutual fund, you actually are investing in a company that is invested in other companies. To make matters worse, a mutual fund, by law, cannot own more than five percent of any company's stock. Now you are once removed and have even less input into the operations of a company. Besides, why would you put your money to work for someone else when you could put it to work for yourself and have direct influence over what happens to it?

Just Don't Take the Risk

I've heard it said that you can take more risk while you are young because you have time to make up for it later on. I wonder who really wants to try making up for losses and mistakes later on instead of just doing it right the first time and watching the money accumulate from day one. Besides, trying to make up for lost time and opportunity only increases the risk of loss when there is less time to do it. It doesn't make sense to me.

Remember, investing doesn't make you an investor; having risk capital, specialized knowledge, and influence over the outcome does. Asset classification before asset allocation will help you determine if your money is investor money, gambler money, or accumulator money. And finally, where you put your money is just as important as the amount of money you have.

It's time to reset our investing presets and get serious about accumulating our money instead of speculating with it.

Activity 8

Are You an Investor?

Asset classification before asset allocation will help you determine if your money is investor money, gambler money, or accumulator money.

1. What portion of your money are you willing to walk away from?
2. What specialized knowledge do you currently have or are willing to study and learn to obtain?
3. In what ways do you have the ability to exercise influence over the outcome with your money?

CHAPTER NINE

Principle #9:

YOU CANNOT SPEND
YOUR WAY TO PROSPERITY.

W hy is it important to understand this principle? To most
people, this concept seems pretty understandable. And
yet, we are told to go out and spend money to stimulate
the economy. We're told to do it for our neighbors. The money we
spend helps to keep them employed. Well, if we really understood this
principle, we would flat out reject this idea.

Spending is consuming, and consuming is not growing wealth
or an economy. Instead, what you get is a short-term surge that will
inevitably collapse after the consumption has taken place. It's like
trying to feed your hunger with cotton candy. You may get a sugar
rush and feel better for a minute, but the short-term good feeling will

soon be followed by a blood sugar crash and leave you feeling worse than you did before the surge.

You Must Save Your Way to Prosperity

Trying to spend your way to prosperity is like trying to overeat your way to skinny. It just isn't going to happen. Instead of trying to spend your way to prosperity, try saving your way there. Sure, there is delayed economic activity while the savings accumulate, but think how much better it will be to build an economy that is sustainable. When you satisfy your hunger with wholesome foods that provide staying power and sustained energy, you find you feel better; you can work and play longer; and you won't feel sick when it's over.

We should focus on growing the economy, not stimulating it. The only way to actually grow an economy is long-term saving. With long-term savings, you provide working capital to grow business. When business grows, the economy grows. With long-term savings, you operate in a cash economy, everything costs less, and the financial risk is substantially lower. The other way, spending, increases the financial dangers and requires that you pay a lot more for everything you buy.

Labor and frugality are the keys to prosperity. If you really want to prosper and grow your economy, accumulate, don't speculate. Learn to work hard and control your appetite. Choose your resources carefully and use them the same way. When you are frugal, you always take care of the most important financial matters first, you follow a carefully laid-out plan, and you make your resources last as long as possible.

There Are Two Kinds of People

When it comes to saving, there are two kinds of people—those who spend first and save if there's anything left over, and those who save first and spend the rest. The important thing to understand is that **spenders always work for savers**. Which kind of person do you want to be? Which kind will grow the economy, and which kind will work to undermine it?

Trying to spend your way to prosperity is really just spending your way into poverty. If you don't have it, don't spend it. If you really need it, save for it. There is no virtue or strength in spending. Strength comes from not giving in to the impulse to spend. Saving is the foundation to financial virtue. Labor and frugality are the keys to prosperity.

So if you really want to prosper, start by saving your way there!

Activity 9
Are You a Saver or a Spender?
Use these questions to take a closer look at your saving and spending habits.

Do you save a set percentage of your income before you spend? If so, how much? If not, how much could you set aside?

Do you spend hard earned money to buy things you don't need just to impress people you don't know or like? Why or why not?

What percentage of your income will you need to save in order to achieve financial prosperity and freedom?

CHAPTER TEN

Principle #10:

YOU CANNOT TREAT
ALL DOLLARS THE SAME.

W hen you treat all dollars the same, you will inevitably end up with the one financial problem and not have the money you need when you need it. You see, when you receive your income, it needs to be divided up into all of the different areas you are responsible for. For example, some of your dollars belong to God (tithes and charitable giving), some belong to the governor (taxes), some belong to the future (emergency and retirement), and the rest belong to the present (living expenses).

Let's take a look at each of these four areas.

The Dollars That Belong to God

Every major religion teaches that the more able have a responsibility to help the less able. In doing so, we are serving God by serving our fellow man. In the Old Testament, Malachi 3:8–10 reads,

> **8** *Will a man rob God? Yet ye have robbed me. But ye say, Wherein have we robbed thee? In tithes and offerings.*
> **9** *Ye are cursed with a curse: for ye have robbed me, even this whole nation.*
> **10** *Bring ye all the tithes into the storehouse, that there may be meat in mine house, and prove me now herewith, saith the Lord of hosts, if I will not open you the windows of heaven, and pour you out a blessing, that there shall not be room enough to receive it.*

When we pay tithes and offerings to God, we make resources available to help the needy and to promote good works among our communities. Caring for the less fortunate is a responsibility that we all share and should be done on a local basis, according to local needs and resources. It is not the job of a government agency. It should also be done by voluntary contributions and never by force. Things don't become important to us until they become personal. Helping solve the problems in our own communities keeps charitable giving personal and productive.

The Dollars That Belong to the Governor

We all benefit from services provided by federal, state, and local government. These benefits have to be paid for. If we are not setting aside part of each dollar to pay for these services, we will have a problem when the tax collector comes knocking at the door. Making sure we set aside a portion of each dollar for the governor makes it possible for us to enjoy benefits together that we could not afford to pay for on our own.

The Dollars That Belong to the Future

What about the future? Who will set aside money for your future? Whose responsibility is it? There are so many demands and so many opportunities to spend all of our money on the present that it takes real discipline to set some aside for the future. But the fact is, no one is going to do it for you. Even a program like Social Security, which was designed to force you to save for the future, is turning out to be a failed idea because the control of your money was turned over to people who spent it on other things. Now, there is nothing left, and every penny of Social Security is spent the second it comes in to pay the benefits promised.

Saving for your future is *your* responsibility. Never trust your future finances to someone else unless you have solid guarantees to back up their promises. If you are going to take risks and try to grow your money faster, be sure to only invest where you can personally use your specialized knowledge and influence so you can mitigate risk and increase your likelihood of success. If you don't have specialized knowledge and the ability to influence the outcome, don't put your money at risk.

People who spend everything on the "here and now" will find they are unprepared for the "then and there." And those of us who have been around a few years can certify that the "then and there" becomes the" here and now" much faster than you would expect.

The Dollars That Belong to the Present

Of course, we need money for the present. Unfortunately, many are spending everything on their current lifestyle and causing a lot of financial wreckage and heartache. In order to separate your dollars into the various areas you are responsible for, you must learn how to put together and follow a spending plan that puts you in charge of your money and lifts you out of financial bondage and into financial freedom.

Learn how to determine the difference between wants and needs. Practice tracking your monthly expenses and become aware of where your money is going. Calculate your future needs to ensure income when you no longer work. Calculate the needs of your loved ones in the event that you are no longer able to provide them. Proper planning and preparation contain the promise of peace of mind.

Activity 10

Dividing Your Dollars[1]

Do you know where each dollar you earn belongs? This activity will help you begin dividing up your dollars so you can put them in the right place.

1. How do you determine the difference between wants and needs?

2. How effective are you at minimizing money spent on wants?

3. Do you follow a spending plan that allows you to have positive surplus cash flow every month? If so, describe it. If not, why not?

4. How do you calculate your future income needs?

5. If you continue to do what you have been doing, will you have the income you need?

6. How do you calculate the income needs of those who depend on you to take care of them?

7. When you die, will your dependents be able to depend on the plans you have in place to take care of them?

---

[1] Not sure where to begin? To learn how to properly divide your dollars, visit www.resetyourbarcode.com. A one-time lifetime membership fee will provide you with access to all the tools you need to predict and plan for your financial future.

CHAPTER ELEVEN

Principle #11:

MONEY DOESN'T CHANGE PEOPLE. IT EXPOSES THEIR VALUES.

W e've all heard stories about people who came into large amounts of money. Whether it came by way of inheritance, lottery, or winning a big contract, it doesn't seem to matter; the result is all too predictable. In far too many cases, money gets blamed for destroying their happiness and ruining their life. The question is, was it the money that changed everything, or did the money simply expose and magnify what was already there? If you look closely into the lives of people who are well-grounded and living compliant with correct financial principles, they don't really change much when they all of a sudden find themselves with substantially more. The extra money simply magnifies and enlarges what they do with the money. On the other hand, people who are not well-grounded in correct principles find many of their weaknesses exposed and magnified when they enjoy increased financial flexibility.

When people are focused on themselves and wanting more, the only thing that usually happens when they get more, especially much more, is they pamper, indulge, and flaunt themselves even more. Why? Because they can, at least for a while—for as everyone knows (but tends to forget), a fool and his money are soon parted.

What Does Your Spending Reveal about You?

My belief is that we are prospered so we can increase our standard of giving, not our standard of living. As with all things, balance is very important. And, of course, giving alone isn't the answer. Giving must be accompanied with training, expectations, and accountability. Nothing is free.

Look around at your personal financial world, and if you are observant and honest with yourself, you will see a reflection of your financial values. You can learn a lot about people by watching what they do with their money. The same is true of you. If you will pay close attention to what you do with every penny, you will expose to yourself what your financial values are.

Be sure to compare your values with financial principles to see if your values are holding you back or helping you succeed. When your values are compliant with principles, you receive a positive consequence. When they are not, you will receive a negative one. The choice is yours.

1. Choose to be a problem-solver and attract the resources to generate wealth.

2. Choose to be a giver. Make sure that your giving creates opportunity and accountability for the receiver, and your giving will generate wealth.
3. Choose to create value before you ask for value.
4. Choose to live in a cash economy as soon as possible and enjoy being free.
5. Choose to plan and prepare so that you will have the money you need when you need it.
6. Choose to preserve capital assets so they can generate income for you.
7. Choose to classify your investments before you diversify them. Never take risk with money you will need.
8. Choose to be an accumulator. The best way to beat inflation is with accumulation, not speculation.
9. Choose to save for the future before using it all in the present. It's your future.
10. Choose to value correct financial principles. Your spending will reflect your values.
11. Choose to be happy. Use your money to buy desired options.
12. Choose the results you want and live the principles that will deliver them.
13. Choose to plan. Hoping is for people who are okay with failure.

Activity 11

Using Your Money to Improve Your World

The way you handle your money exposes your values. How would you use an increase in money to make the world better?

1. If you suddenly found yourself with substantially more money than you need, how would you use it to solve problems?

2. What problems would you try to solve first?

3. What problems are you working to solve with the money you have now?

CHAPTER TWELVE

Principle #12:

MONEY DOESN'T BUY HAPPINESS. IT BUYS OPTIONS.

Happiness is a choice; it cannot be purchased. That being said, there are still a lot of people who believe that if they just had more money or more "stuff," they would be happy.

There are studies that suggest that a certain amount of money increases happiness. Once that number is surpassed, the extra money actually causes happiness to decrease. I wonder, is it the money that causes the increase and then the decrease in happiness, or is it something else?

Money Buys Options

I believe that the real issue isn't money but rather the feeling of well-being and control over one's life and circumstances that having enough money provides. So, the real issue is control. Having money gives us some control over our circumstances. With that perceived control comes the feeling of well-being and happiness. It's ironic that too much money tends to give more options, and with more options comes the feeling of being out of control. Instead of quality and simplicity of life, you experience more quantity and complexity.

So happiness isn't something you can purchase with money, but money can purchase options. It is these options that give you the feeling of power or influence over your life. A feeling of power and influence brings a sense of happiness. Please don't misunderstand; I'm not saying that money isn't important, because it is. What I am saying is that if your focus is on money, happiness may be very elusive. But if you focus on the things that make you truly happy and work to have enough money to make them available, you will be much happier.

What Money Can Buy

Consider some of the options that money can buy … and what it can't.

1. Money can't buy good health, but it can buy good health care.
2. Money can't buy great relationships, but it can buy resources that allow you time and tools to develop and strengthen those relationships.
3. Money can't buy time, but it can buy flexibility for how you spend your time.
4. Money can't buy knowledge or wisdom, but it can buy books to read and provide opportunities to experience life and gain wisdom.

5. Money can't buy loyalty, but it can buy resources that demonstrate your support and commitment, which in turn earn loyalty.

6. Money can't buy love, but it can buy expressions of the love you feel for others.

Hopefully, you get the idea. Money itself is a tool, a resource to help us fulfill our dreams and our highest purpose, which is where happiness comes from.

Remember, money doesn't buy happiness; it buys options. Happiness is a choice. It cannot be purchased.

Activity 12
What Kind of Happiness Does Your Money Buy?
This activity will help you determine whether money really makes you happy.

1. Do you see money as the source of your happiness or as a resource to give you options?

2. Do you choose to be happy and to use money to continually improve the quality of life for yourself and those around you? Why or why not?

3. Why is money important to you?

4. What are the top 5 things you will do with money to improve happiness for yourself and others?

CHAPTER THIRTEEN

Principle #13:

MONEY IS SUBJECT TO THE "LAW OF THE HARVEST."

T he "Law of the Harvest" states that you reap what you sow. I have learned by firsthand experience that this is true. Growing up working for farmers in Idaho taught me several things about the "Law of the Harvest" that I later discovered also apply to money. I would like to discuss the following three elements of the "Law of the Harvest."

You Reap What You Sow

First is what I call the "like kind" element. The **"like kind" element** suggests that whatever you plant, that is what you will harvest. If you sow peas, you will reap peas. If you sow potatoes, you will reap potatoes. You cannot sow corn and reap broccoli instead. The laws of nature do not allow this. Wouldn't it be confusing if natural law allowed for one thing to be planted and then something entirely different to grow for the harvest? The great benefit to knowing about this element of the "Law of the Harvest" is that with a little forethought, you can select what you want to reap, and that will tell you what you need to sow. This element of predictability allows us to make plans with a high degree of confidence about what to expect as an outcome.

Money also operates using the "like kind" element of the "Law of the Harvest." You see, if you sow safety, you reap predictability. If you sow risk, you reap uncertainty. If you sow small amounts, you are likely to reap insufficient funds. If you sow overspending, you will reap dependency. If you sow debt, you will reap diminished rewards for your labor and a loss of economic freedom.

The "like kind" element of the "Law of the Harvest" tells you what you are going to reap based upon what you sow. **Choose carefully what you sow**.

Accumulating Wealth Takes Time

Second is what I call the "growing season" element. The **"growing season" element** teaches that different crops require different growing seasons. In other words, you must expect a certain length of time between sowing and reaping. For example, if you want to eat leafy greens, you will need approximately forty to fifty-five days between planting and harvesting. So, at the right time of year and in the right location, you can plant things like spinach and lettuce, and within forty to fifty-five days, you can enjoy your harvest.

However, if you are trying to grow a Chinese bamboo tree, it will require more patience. You see, the Chinese bamboo tree appears to lie dormant in the ground for 4 years, not giving any evidence that it is ever going to do anything. Then, dramatically, in the fifth year, it shoots up through the earth and reaches a height of approximately eighty feet. What would happen if you tried to harvest the Chinese bamboo tree in year three or four? Obviously, the result would be disastrous.

Money is also subject to a "growing season." Accumulating wealth or growing money takes time. How big do you want your money tree to be? What are the future needs you are preparing for? You have to expect an appropriate period of waiting. If you try to condense the growing season into too short a time period, you may end up destroying the entire harvest.

Remember the Rule of 72 referenced earlier in Chapter Six? It takes a substantial amount of time to grow financial independence. And keep in mind that the Rule of 72 does not take into account the damaging effect of taxes or the positive effect of additional contributions to your savings. If you try to rush your harvest by taking inappropriate risk, you run a major risk of being worse off than if you just keep what you have. Always give yourself time to observe the proper growing season.

That being said, consider how long it will likely take to grow your money to full maturity. In other words, plan a harvest substantial enough to sustain you through the winter years of your life.

Suppose you are saving $500.00 per month and earning 3% interest on your account.[2] After saving for 25 years, you could expect your account to grow to approximately $223,000.00. That's a lot of money! However, if you turn that into a monthly income using the same 3% interest rate, you would only receive about $557.00 each month. It's not my intent to diminish the value of $557.00, but at today's cost of living, that wouldn't even come close to being enough to cover living expenses, even if you didn't have a mortgage payment.

---

2   At the time of this writing, guaranteed rates at the bank are very low, and a person would be hard-pressed to find an account paying 3%. But for our example, let's suppose that over the long term, a 3% average is achievable.

Using the Rule of 72 and a realistic rate of return can give you a good indication of how much you will need to save every month to grow the harvest you need. The more time you have and the more you save, the better your chances of reaching your objective. Unfortunately, far too many Americans are trying to take shortcuts and rush the growing season. This goes against the "Law of the Harvest" and will undermine your financial success. If you are simply growing leafy greens or an emergency fund, the growing season may only take a short while. However, if you are trying to grow a financial Chinese bamboo tree, you had better give it the time it needs to fully mature.

Caring for Your "Crop"

The third element in the "Law of the Harvest" is the **T.L.C.**, which stands for tender loving care. Simply scattering a few seeds here and there at the beginning of the season doesn't guarantee a bountiful harvest. In fact, it is highly doubtful that there will be any harvest at all. Chances are great that scorching sun, lack of water, and choking weeds will prevent any seed from taking root and bearing fruit.

If you want a bountiful harvest when it comes time to reap, you must not only apply tender loving care when the seeds are sown, but also throughout the entire time you want your plants to grow. Every good gardener will prepare the soil, sow the seeds, properly water, allow plenty of sunshine, and keep the area weed free.

This third element of the "Law of the Harvest" applies to money as well. You cannot simply save a few dollars here and there and expect to have enough to supply your future needs. First, you must understand the laws that govern economic freedom. Learning the governing laws is like preparing the soil. Second, you must prepare a well-thought-out plan. Preparing a plan is like choosing what kind of seed to plant so you will know what kind of harvest to expect. Third, you must follow the plan. Following the plan is like making sure that your plants get plenty of water and sunshine. Fourth, you must review and update your plan every year so that it is kept up-to-date. Reviewing and updating your plan is like keeping your garden weed-free.

Since you will reap what you sow, it makes good sense to sow what you want to reap; give your money the time it needs to mature, and give it proper maintenance so that you will have an abundant harvest.

Remember, money is subject to the "Law of the Harvest."

Activity 13

Planning for Your Future Financial "Harvest"

Use the rules of the "Law of the Harvest" to begin crafting a financial plan for your future.

1. Summarize the governing laws of finance and economics.
2. What do you think is a realistic long-term rate of return?
3. How much are you saving each month? How much should you be saving?
4. Describe your carefully crafted retirement savings plan[3] (or, an ideal plan you would like to follow). How are you implementing it, and how often will you review it and make necessary adjustments?

---

3   To learn how to create a retirement savings plan, visit www.resetyourbarcode.com. A one-time lifetime membership fee will provide you with access to all the tools you need to predict and plan for your financial future.

CHAPTER FOURTEEN

Principle #14:

HOPING IS NOT PLANNING.

A simple definition of **financial planning** is deciding what you can live without today so you will know what you will have to live with tomorrow.

Many people make financial planning way more complicated than it needs to be, and way too expensive, for that matter. I know, because for years, I was as guilty as anyone. I spent large sums of money to purchase comprehensive planning software and then charged a substantial amount of money to create sophisticated plans for people. Here's the bad news: the plan never, and I mean *never*, works out the way it is projected to. So here's a pretty good question. Why would you pay a lot of money for a plan that will not turn out the way it says it will? Now, here's the good news. You don't have to.

One of the reasons that traditional financial plans haven't worked out the way they forecasted is because they were built on hoped-for projections rather than guaranteed projections. For example, most plans use assumptions about rate of return, inflation, and taxation. When have we ever been able to control rate of return? Never! How about inflation? Is that something you can control? Nope! Well what about taxes? How is that working out?

When we construct a plan based on things we hope will happen instead of things we can plan on, we have a financial hope, not a financial plan.

What You *Can* Control

Think about the things you can actually control relative to your finances. There are only three of them. **One, you can control how long you work**. If you earn a large income and save enough of it, you may be able to retire earlier than someone who doesn't. If you don't have a large income and/or you don't save enough, you may have to work longer. Still, the decision is yours. How long are you going to work? Some might argue that death and or disability may cut your working years short, but I contend that you can purchase protection that provides income replacement in those cases, and so you still have some control over how long you are going to work.

Two, you can control what percentage of your income you save. Even though this pill is a difficult one to swallow, spending has much more to do with the amount you save than your income does. I know people who save a pretty good chunk of a very modest income and others who save very little of their large income. The key to saving is spending (less).

Three, you can control where you put your money. Successfully growing your money begins with putting it in the right place in the first place. As I discussed earlier, it is important to classify your money before you diversify it. What kind of money is it? Is it investor, gambler, or accumulator money? Knowing this up front will help shape your expectations for how long it will take to grow your money—or your expectations for whether it will grow at all.

Make a Year-by-Year Plan

How often do circumstances in your life change and cause you to change your expectations? If you are anything like me, it happens all the time. If that is the case, how useful is a twenty, thirty, or forty-year plan? It's not. So rather than make an extended plan, **plan one year at a time**. That's right, one year at a time. Sure, you can forecast out into the future to get an estimate of how things will look down the road, but remember, things will change. So after you forecast ahead, make sure that you re-forecast each and every year.

There are at least two great benefits of planning year-to-year. First, **you keep your expectations much more realistic** because you are adjusting annually to the changes in your life. This is really helpful because you don't end up with an unpleasant surprise and not enough time to adjust to it. Second, **it keeps your objectives realistic**. In other words, we can all set an objective or goal for a year and accomplish it. Even if we fail to reach our goal, we have only lost one year instead of a decade. One year at a time seems to be pretty manageable for most people and prevents becoming overwhelmed. When people become overwhelmed, they tend to give up, and that will definitely cost them valuable time.

So to make sure you are putting together a financial plan instead of a financial hope. Be sure to base it on things you can control, namely, how long you will work, how much you will save, and where you will put your hard-earned money. Then, be sure you reset your plan every year.

Remember, hoping is not planning. Is your plan something you can plan on? Complete Activity 14, and you will be on your way to creating a reliable, effective financial plan. When changes come, adjust. It's always easier to adjust a plan than it is to operate without one in the first place.

Activity 14

Starting a Year-by-Year Plan

This activity puts you on the path to creating a financial plan and achieving financial freedom.

1. When do you need to be financially free?
2. Write down the five most important things for which you want to have money (such as retirement, education, family fun, etc.).
3. What will you do this year to make sure that you will have the money when you need it?

CHAPTER FIFTEEN

CONSTRUCTING A PLAN USING THE "FIVE DEGREES OF FINANCIAL FREEDOM"

I t's time to construct a financial plan to freedom. For some, the thought of actually being financially free is so far away because they will have to pay for their children's education, pay for their weddings, pay for their mortgage, etc. It seems so far away—and in many cases so impossible—that many people become overwhelmed and give up on the whole idea. Doing nothing—even for a while—is extremely threatening to your financial success because you take away so much valuable and necessary time from your financial growing season.

Others view financial freedom as an event and keep waiting to get started because of current pressing needs. Still others don't want to do what it takes and would rather hope for a miracle, like winning the lottery or some kind of sweepstakes that will solve all their financial problems. Of course, the only real way to take control and make it happen is to get started today.

When you construct your financial plan, be sure to follow the "Five Degrees of Financial Freedom." This is absolutely critical.

The "First Degree"

Stage 1: Establish and follow a spending plan that provides you with surplus cash flow each and every month.

Instead of being "restricted" by a budget, you will actually experience tremendous freedom as you experience progress toward your goal every month. Think of how a kite works. Without any kind of anchor at the end of the kite string, the kite will fly itself right into the ground. With an appropriate anchor, the kite is allowed to soar as high as the string is long.

So rather than think of a spending plan as restrictive or confining, think of it as the anchor that will allow your financial plan to soar, and then feed it the string it needs to go higher as fast as you can. When you establish and follow a well-thought-out spending plan, you will experience the first degree of financial freedom. The first degree must be achieved before you can advance to the second degree.

The "Second Degree"

Stage 2: Evaluate your needs and purchase critical protection.

So, what is protection and what is critical protection? Protection is what I call **money on demand**. It is money that shows up at the very time it is needed, such as life, disability, and health insurance benefits. There are many other kinds of insurance, such as auto, home, liability, etc. All these provide protection. But **critical protection** provides money on demand for those things that are the most difficult, if not impossible, to overcome. For example, if I bought a new car and then wrecked it, I would experience a troubling setback. However, with time, I could probably overcome it as long as I have the ability to continue working.

The most critical protections are the ones that cover me when my ability to get back to work is taken from me, such as death or permanent disability. The beauty of these tools is that they can be purchased for pennies on the dollar. By setting aside a small portion of your spending plan to pay for money that shows up when it is needed most, you experience the second degree of financial freedom.

You will be amazed at how much freedom you experience just knowing that you have made provision for some of the most critical threats to your family's financial security. If today is the day that you get kicked off the planet, you can be assured that the dollars you purchased with pennies will show up and complete the plan you were not able to. That's freedom!

The "Third Degree"

Stage 3: Systematically accumulate money for emergencies and opportunities.

The next stage requires that you build what I call **the E&O account**. E&O stands for emergency and opportunity. Without a sufficient emergency and opportunity fund, you run a very high risk of being plunged into further debt. Since financial and economic freedom is our purpose, let's discuss how the E&O savings account operates and helps us achieve freedom.

First, let's talk about the emergency portion of the account. Too often, people use this emergency portion as an extension to their checking account. When they do this, they don't really have an emergency fund but rather an overdraft to cover overspending. The primary purpose of the emergency portion of your E&O fund is to provide for the major emergency of not being able to produce income. **The emergency fund is a short-term income replacement fund.**

So how large should it be? Well, that depends on your personal circumstances. A good rule of thumb is to have a minimum of six months' worth of living expenses set aside so that you could weather a temporary layoff or transition period between employments. It takes some real discipline and effort to accumulate that amount of money and to leave it alone, but if you will make saving from every paycheck a priority and automatic habit, it will happen.

Second is the opportunity portion of your savings. **The opportunity fund handles financial surprises and preplanned expenses**, such as car repairs, an insurance deductible or co-pay, or even something fun, like a vacation. One of the great benefits of having an opportunity fund is when the time is right, you will be able to take lump sums and make important purchases, pay off debt, or make investments for the future. That's why it's called opportunity money, so you can take advantage of great opportunities when they come along. Too often, opportunities come and go, and their benefits are realized by someone else because we haven't prepared to take advantage of them.

Through consistent saving and planned spending, you will eventually have money for emergencies and opportunities.

The "Fourth Degree"

Stage 4: Accelerate debt reduction.

In this stage, you really start seeing the benefits of your effort and discipline. This is where financial freedom begins to happen exponentially. If you have followed each stage up to now, you are in a position to concentrate full effort in to getting out of debt. When I say out of debt, I mean *all debt*, including your mortgage. Stop and imagine the power and freedom that you will enjoy when the only expenses you have are for maintenance. A person with no debt can survive on very little income if they have to. Surviving isn't our objective, but my point is **when you are debt-free, you have lots of options**.

When you focus on debt reduction, try a process I call "worst first." When you think of your worst debts you may consider the largest one to be the worst one. However, **your worst debt is the one that you are paying the highest interest on**. Systematically take chunks of your opportunity fund and pay off the worst debt.

One of the best investments you will ever make is to pay off debt. The reason for this is because debt works the Rule of 72 against you. Instead of benefits compounding in your favor at the end of the growth period, with debt, all of the cost and damage caused by interest is worse at the beginning and only gets better slowly toward the end of the loan. For this reason, you will want to get rid of debt and its accompanying interest as soon as possible.

When the worst loan is paid, you are now free to take the money you were using to pay it and the money you are using to service the next one and "double down." To "**double down**," use the money that was paying down the first debt and add it to the payment on the next debt to pay it off even faster. As each loan is paid, you free up more money to go after the next debt and accelerate the rate of payoff as you go. Sooner than you may have ever thought possible, you will be living the debt-free life.

Some people say that there is good debt and bad debt. I say there is freedom and there is debt. True, some debt is worse than other debt, but I don't believe there is such a thing as good debt.

The "Fifth Degree"

Stage 5: Grow your wealth.

Step by step, you have been achieving financial freedom by degrees. With your debt paid off, you are ready to go after the fifth degree and enjoy financial and economic freedom to its fullest. You are now ready to grow your money.

I realize that you may have some money growing already because of an employer-sponsored retirement plan or something of that nature. But now you are ready to go beyond the usual watered-down effort that most people give to growing their financial freedom. Now you can take chunks from your opportunity fund and apply it to opportunities you have prepared yourself to recognize and take advantage of.

As you continue to follow the five stages outlined above, you will have money you can invest for the long haul where it can get better returns and enjoy available tax-preferred treatment. When invested properly, your money will grow, and each new growth will cause more growth and result in a compounding effect until the principal is large enough to provide income even if you are no longer working. Now that's freedom!

There are only two ways to generate income, and you have put yourself in the enviable position of being able to choose whether you want to continue working or not. At this point, work is all about contribution rather than necessity. You are now free to focus more and more on the things that are the most important to you.

Congratulations, you now hold the fifth degree in financial freedom!

Activity 15

Achieving the Five Degrees of Financial Freedom

Answering the following questions will help you thoughtfully move through each stage and achieve the five degrees of financial freedom.

1. Does your spending plan provide you with surplus cash flow for saving every month? If so, how much more could or should it be?

2. Do you have the most important protection in place, such as protection on your income-producing ability, and do you have sufficient amounts? How much capital do you think it would take to replace your income indefinitely?

3. Do you have an emergency and opportunity account? Is it fully funded? How much should you have in that account to handle emergencies and opportunities?

4. If you have debt, make a list of everything you owe and prioritize it based on highest to lowest interest. Place the worst first.

5. Classify your growth money. Is it investor, accumulator, or gambler money? What specialized knowledge do you have or need to get? How will you be able to influence the outcome of your investments?

6. How soon are you ready to get started on your financial freedom plan?

Section Two

THREE WAKE-UP CALLS

In this section, you'll learn how to complete the second step in resetting your financial barcode, Step 2—"The Ebenezer Experience." This step will alert you to changes you can make now to make your future financial situation more secure.

In "The Ebenezer Experience," you will be given three wakeup calls to help you get on track and keep you on track, financially speaking. If you take charge today, you won't be disappointed tomorrow.

The three wakeup calls are

1. **Take the Wants vs. Needs Test.**
2. **Track your spending.**
3. **Forecast survivor income.**

THE SECOND STEP, OR "THE EBENEZER EXPERIENCE"

Ebenezer Scrooge of Charles Dickens' classic *A Christmas Carol* started out as a pretty good guy with talent and good intentions. However, over time, greed, bitterness, and distrust so clouded his way of thinking that they overshadowed his whole existence. Before long,  the only thing that mattered to him was earning and keeping as much money as he could. Blinded by his new false and corrupted values, he was creating a life story with a very unhappy ending.

As his story goes, he was visited by his former business partner who tried to warn him of the consequences and heavy burden he would carry with him into the afterlife unless he changed his ways. Following the warning of Jacob Marley, Scrooge received the visitations of three Christmas spirits who gave him the chance of a lifetime, an opportunity to see past himself and change his outlook. Scrooge was offered a wakeup call and a chance to turn his life around before it was everlastingly too late.

To his good credit, even though it took some serious effort on the part of the Christmas spirits, Ebenezer saw the light. When he did, he recognized that his past created his present and what he was now doing was creating his future. The benefit of seeing the future he was creating gave him great motivation and caused him to ask with tremendous anguish of soul, "Is it everlastingly too late to change? Or is there still time to make amends?"

When the Spirits left, Scrooge found himself a new creature. His desire to make the future better gave him a new heart and a new vision of what could be. Everything changed. He was kinder to everyone, including his employee. He looked for ways to use his money to make life better for others. In the end, what he was really doing was making life better for himself.

I call this step "The Ebenezer Experience" because most of us need a similar kind of wakeup call. Ebenezer's experience is a good representation of what happens to us when we allow our values to become corrupted. It's true in finances as well as in other areas of our life.

So what does Ebenezer's experience have to do with you and your financial plan? Well, first, it illustrates very well why it is so important to be sure your financial values are compatible with correct financial principles. Remember, principles are the gatekeepers; until you comply, you shall not pass and receive a positive consequence. And second, you, too, can receive a wakeup call relative to what you are doing with your money. As I help people do their planning I am amazed at how many cannot give an accurate accounting of where their money goes. Many have no idea.

In Section Two, I am going to share three things you can do as you plan your future finances. These actions will help you know where your money is going, make informed decisions about where you want it to go, and project into the future what you will need and what it will take to get you there.

CHAPTER SIXTEEN

Wake-Up Call #1:

TAKE THE WANTS
VS. NEEDS TEST.

H ere is how it works. Before you spend any money or make a purchase, ask yourself these three questions.

- Do I have the cash?
- Will it add quality and simplicity, or quantity and complexity to my life?
- Is this the best use of my resources?

Question One: Do I Have the Cash?

If you don't have the cash, you should not make the purchase. If you do, you'll plunge yourself into a credit economy and run the very high risk of paying way more than you should for nearly everything you buy.

You will also substantially increase the risk of financial loss. I've seen many times where income has gone away, but the debt never does. The resulting stress can rob you of happiness and your most important relationships. Sometimes people think they can find relief from heavy burdens of debt by declaring bankruptcy, only to find that they really just passed their burden on to others and increased the cost of living in the process.

Remember the old saying, "You can pay me now or you can pay me later, but you've got to pay me"? Even though it may not seem like it at the time, it is so much easier to save before you spend and avoid a lot of possible complications. So, before you spend money, make sure you have the cash!

Question Two: Will It Add Quality and Simplicity, or Quantity and Complexity to My Life?

How many times have you worked hard, saved money, and made a purchase that you believed would solve all your problems and make life sweet, only to find that many of the things you own actually end up owning you? What you expected to enrich your life by adding quality and simplicity ended up giving you more quantity and complexity instead.

For example, many of us dream of having a larger home with a bigger yard only to find that property taxes, along with maintenance time and costs, become more than we bargained for. Or what about that fancy car? The same rules often apply. Besides cars and homes, there are many time-saving devices that are worth their weight in gold. However, be careful that your newfound free time doesn't get swallowed up working more so you can afford to purchase more time-saving devices. You don't have to look very far to see where that road will lead.

Leonardo Da Vinci is quoted as saying, "Simplicity is the ultimate sophistication." I believe that to be true. In my own experience, I found that I could have had a lot of fun with just a baseball, a bat, and a baseball glove, if I only had the time to use them. I was too busy paying for, insuring, servicing, and storing motorcycles, snowmobiles, and other toys. It took a while, but I eventually discovered that I could enjoy more quality and simplicity by really focusing my efforts and pleasures in a few areas because now I actually had time to use them. If your purchase adds quality and simplicity to your life, it will be long enjoyed. If it brings quantity and complexity, your enjoyment may be short-lived. Always ask yourself, "Am I adding quality and simplicity?"

Question Three: Is This the Best Use of My Resources?

How many people do you know who are pretty good about saving first and only spending money on things that seem pretty sensible, but have neither an emergency fund nor sufficient resources accumulating for their future? If you are not setting money aside for your own future needs, who will? Who is going to bail you out in your time of need? Maybe you have a rich and generous uncle just waiting to bestow untold wealth on you, but most people don't. In fact, almost no one does.

Because you are primarily responsible for your own future financial security, it's a great idea to always ask if a purchase fits into and supports your financial plan. If it doesn't, maybe the purchase should be avoided. When our focus is always on the here and now, we usually find ourselves unprepared for the then and there. A good financial plan that takes into consideration both the future and the present will help you maintain a balanced perspective so you know how much of your income to use now and how much to set aside for later.

I have had clients ask me all kinds of questions about potential purchases (as though they needed my permission) such as, "With all this money, shouldn't I be spending more?" or, "Do you think I can afford to buy this boat or cabin?" My response is pretty much always the same.

To the question, "Shouldn't I be spending this money?" I ask, "What would you like to be doing that you are not already?" Most of the time, the answer was, "Nothing, really. I already travel as much as I want and play golf almost every day." Then my answer is no. You don't spend money just because you have it. Money is to be used to generate wealth, not to consume it.

For the person who asks, "Can I afford to make this purchase?" I ask, "Do you have the cash? Will this purchase add quality and simplicity? Is it the best use of your resources?" If you can answer affirmatively to those three questions, then I say go for it. If not, maybe you should reconsider if the purchase is in your best interest.

One of my clients wondered whether he could buy a boat. As we went through the questions, it was obvious they had saved up the cash; that was good. The answer to the quality and simplicity question was a big yes on the quality part because it was an activity that the whole family enjoyed, and it would give them a fun reason to spend time together. The simplicity question gave him reason to pause because everybody knows that boat ownership is not about simplicity; however, he felt that the hassle was justified, and I agreed. When we came to the best use of resources question, he asked what I meant. I simply reminded him that he had put together a financial plan that required him to save pretty aggressively because of a late start. Then I asked if this purchase would throw off his plan, and if so, was he prepared to work longer and or save even more to make up for the money spent on a boat. Of course, it was his money and he could have easily bought the new boat, but on reflection of his own established priorities, he decided he wasn't willing to void his financial plan, and he held on to his money.

My point is not to tell people what they can and cannot do. It is to help them make sure that they really want to do what they are considering. **When we say yes to one thing, we are always saying no to something else, and when we say no to something, we are saying yes to something else**. My goal is help you make a choice you are happy to live with.

Use the Wants vs. Needs Test, and you may surprise yourself when you discover how often you spend money based on emotion rather than logic.

Activity 16

Take the Wants vs. Needs Test

Think about your last significant purchase. Was it based on emotion or logic? The Wants vs. Needs Test will help you figure that out.

1. What was your last significant purchase?
2. Did you have the cash?
3. Did it add quality and simplicity, or quantity and complexity to your life?
4. Was this the best use of your resources?
5. After asking the three questions in the Wants vs. Needs Test, would you have still bought the item?

CHAPTER SEVENTEEN

Wake-Up Call #2:

TRACK YOUR SPENDING.

ccountability requires honesty and bravery. Are you brave enough and honest enough to track where all of your money is going? For many of us, there is a substantial amount of spending that goes unaccounted for. As long as we don't know where it's going, we cannot take control and make it go where it matters most. How much more could you save if you knew what you were spending on unnecessary things? In my experience, those who track their spending save more.

Throughout my years of advising people how to plan their finances so they can finance their plans, I've been surprised at how some can save big on a small income and some with a big income cannot even save a small amount. What is the difference? Those who save big on small incomes know where every penny is going. And those with big incomes who can't save a small amount usually can't tell you where all the money goes. So what is the difference? Tracking spending!

Here is a live example of what I'm talking about. Couple #1 is retired and has a very modest income and lifestyle to go with it. Every so often, they call and make arrangements to increase their savings. Couple #2 is also retired and has an annual income more than twice the size of couple #1, and once or twice per year, they call me to see if they can get more. Of course, I tell them they can, but I also point out that they are spending down their principal, and their money might not last as long as they do. Upon inspection to see if they really need the money, they always confess that they don't know where it all goes.

I am confident that if they would take the small amount of time required to track and account for all of their spending, they would have an "Ebenezer Experience." In other words, they would be surprised just how much is being spent on something that doesn't matter as much as they think it does. Now, I'm not saying they shouldn't spend the money. They can do what they want; it's theirs. What I'm trying to say is if they would track it and be aware of it, they would be able to decide for themselves whether or not it's worth it.

The 80/20 Rule

Have you ever heard of the 80/20 Rule? This simple rule suggests that **20% of activity is responsible for 80% of results**. It can also be reversed to say that sometimes 80% of activity is responsible for only 20% of productivity. In this case, 80% of spending is only providing 20% of the benefit being enjoyed. Said another way, approximately 20% of the money you spend is producing close to 80% of the enjoyment you receive. That being said, it makes very good sense to track all spending and see if it's being spent where it will do the most good.

Have you ever spent a lot of money only to receive modest pleasure compared to a seemingly small purchase that provided you with immense enjoyment? If so, you've experienced the 80/20 rule.

How Do I Begin?

So, how do you track your expenses? There are several ways; use the one that works best for you. You can keep a pencil and pad with you at all times and simply record every purchase. You can keep notes on your smart phone. You can also use your debit or credit card for every purchase, no matter how small.

At the end of the month, make a notation next to every purchase with an N indicating it was a need and a W indicating it was a want. Be sure to use the Wants vs. Needs Test to make your distinction. If you do this simple process for a couple of months, you will be aware and amazed to find out just what you are spending your money on, and odds are very high you will be able to find some money that could be spent more wisely—or better still, put into savings.

Benjamin Franklin said, "A penny saved is a penny earned." That is especially true if that penny earns interest and gives you another penny. And the pennies do add up.

Activity 17

Track Your Spending

Knowing where every penny goes can make a difference. These questions will help you learn how to track your expenses.

1. Hold yourself accountable. List the last five most recent purchases and label them according to whether they were wants or needs.
2. How much, if any, could have been saved rather than spent?
3. List three things you can and will do to improve your spending and saving habits.
4. Which tracking system will work best for you?

CHAPTER EIGHTEEN

Wake-Up Call #3:

FORECAST SURVIVOR INCOME.

T his wakeup call gives you an "Ebenezer Experience" by giving you a glimpse into your financial future to see if you like it. I'm not talking about gazing into a crystal ball; however, it is surprising just how clearly you can predict future outcomes by examining present behavior and forecasting it into the future.

Just as Ebenezer Scrooge visited his future and saw the results he was creating based upon his present behavior, you too can visit the future by forecasting the value of your current assets and regular savings. The good news is that, one year at a time, you can shape your future by taking charge of your present.

How Do I Make a Future Financial Forecast?

A future financial forecast can be completed manually using a financial formula and calculator.[4] I call this financial forecast "Calculating Survivor Income." First, you calculate the income you will have if you survive to old age. Second, you calculate the income you will leave to your dependents if you don't survive. Let's take a look.

Calculate Future Monthly Income

1. Take the current value of any income-producing assets and calculate the future value of those assets at the time you would like to see, such as at age 65. For example,

401K = $100,000
IRA = $50,000 } Add all your income-producing assets.
Total = $150,000

Grow $150,000 @ 3% for 25 years } Multiply the total by the **expected growth rate** and **number of years** of growth.

Total Expected Future Value = $314,066 } Calculate total value of assets at age 65.

2. Now take the amount you are currently saving in long-term growth accounts (such as 401k or IRA) and calculate the future value of your savings.

---

4   To use an online calculator, go to www.resetyourbarcode.com. This membership-based website provides a Financial Reset Calculator to make the forecasting process quick and easy. It also makes a very nice, one-page annual financial plan.

$500 per month ⎤⊢ Amount saved monthly.

$500 per month for 25 years @ 3% ⎤⊢ Multiply amount by **number of years** of savings and **expected growth rate.**

Total Expected Future Value = $223,003 ⎤⊢ Calculate total savings at age 65.

3. Add the future value of your current assets and the future value of your savings.

Future Current Assets = $314,066
Future Savings = $223,003
Total Future Assets = $537,069

⎤⊢ Add total future assets at age 65.

4. Because you plan to live on the interest your assets yield, calculate that annual interest amount next. Multiply the total of your total future assets by a current safe money interest rate to see how much income your assets would produce annually.

$537,069 x 3% = $16,112 annually ⎤⊢ Calculate annual earned interest.

5. Now divide the total annual interest by twelve and you have a picture of your future monthly income.

$16,112 / 12 = $1,342 monthly ⎤⊢ Calculate monthly income.

If the number makes you question how you will be able to get by, then ask yourself what can be done *now* to cause a better outcome *then.*

Remember, the things you can control are **working longer; saving more**; and **putting your money in the right place in the first place**.

Calculate Survivor Income

Now let's calculate the income that your dependents will have to survive on in case you are not there to support them.

1. Add up all current life insurance benefits.

Total Life insurance Benefits = $500,00]- Add life insurance benefits.

2. Add all current income-producing assets and combine with life insurance.

Life insurance Benefits = $500,000
Income-Producing Assets = $150,000   ]- Add life insurance and other assets.
Total Assets = $650,000

3. Add up all debt and subtract from total assets.

Total Assets = $650,000
Total Debt = -$220,000   ]- Subtract total debt from total assets.
Total Remaining Assets = $430,000

4. Multiply the net balance by a current safe money interest rate to arrive at the annual income that will be available.

$430,000 x 3% = $12,900 annually]- Calculate annual earned interest.

5. Divide the annual income by twelve.

12,900 / 12 = $1,075 monthly   ]- Calculate survivor monthly income.

Now you will have a good picture of the monthly income available to your survivors. The question is, how well will they be able to survive? If the answer causes you or your survivors concern, ask yourself, "What can I do now to improve the outcome?" The only thing you can control in this situation is how much life insurance you own. **If you want**

more life insurance, apply for it now. Life insurance is one of those things that you can only get when you don't need it. Once you need it, it's too late.

Taking a look into your financial future based upon the way you are living your financial present is very effective. You should feel optimistic because you are taking action while you still have time to change the outcome. It worked for Ebenezer, and it will work for you.

Activity 18

Forecast Survivor Income

Use the financial formula and calculator in Chapter Eighteen to forecast your financial future.

1. How much income will you need to survive?
2. Complete the steps for calculating future monthly income. How much will you have if you don't make any changes?
3. Complete the steps for calculating survivor income. How much survivor income will be available for your dependents?
4. What changes, if any, do you need to make to your current financial plan?

THREE LESSONS TO LEARN

In this section, you'll learn how to complete the third step in resetting your financial barcode, Step 3—"The Wooden Puppet Experience." In this step, you will learn how to create a very simple, effective, one-page, personalized, annual financial plan, one you can live with and succeed with.

"The Wooden Puppet Experience" step teaches that financial success cannot be quickly or easily achieved. It takes great personal discipline and sacrifice. You can learn these lessons through the school of hard knocks, or you can learn from the experiences of others and avoid painful missteps. In this section, you'll learn three lessons that will help you reset your financial barcode and put you on the path to achieving financial freedom.

The three lessons are

1. There are no shortcuts.
2. Nothing is free.
3. Everyone must face Monstro.

At the end of this section, you'll learn the five phases of building a solid financial plan. Putting together an annual financial plan is best accomplished by moving through each of the five phases in order, setting priorities that you will accomplish year-to-year.

THE THIRD STEP, OR "THE WOODEN PUPPET EXPERIENCE"

Who is your favorite wooden puppet and why? Is it Pinocchio? What parts of Pinocchio's story do you find memorable? Is it because he had a dream and worked to make it come true? Is it because his nose grew every time he told a lie?  For most of us, what we remember most about Pinocchio is that he wanted to become "a real boy."

In other words, Pinocchio wanted freedom from external strings or controls. In order to take control and get rid of the strings, he needed to learn how to handle the responsibilities of freedom, for only then could he have it. As instructed by the Blue Fairy, Pinocchio would have to become truthful, brave, and unselfish. Only then would he become "a real boy" and enjoy freedom.

As you know, freedom always comes at a price and is never free. In fact, nothing is! In his efforts to become "a real boy," Pinocchio found that earning freedom takes hard work and sacrifice, and the path is fraught with danger. He made many mistakes along the way, and yet with each one, he gained knowledge and experience that would ultimately set him free. He became "a real boy," and *you can, too.*

Becoming "a real boy" financially speaking also takes hard work and sacrifice, and like Pinocchio's journey, it is fraught with potential risks. However, there are specific things you can do that will greatly improve your likelihood of success and shorten the time it takes you to achieve true financial freedom.

Before we proceed to the planning steps that will allow you to achieve financial freedom, let's review a few lessons Pinocchio learned so that we can benefit from his experience. By the way, I've heard it said that experience is the best teacher; however, she also charges the highest tuition. Learning from the experience of others will substantially reduce the cost of your education. So, let's see what we can learn from Pinocchio's experience.

CHAPTER NINETEEN

The First Lesson:

THERE ARE NO SHORTCUTS.

In this first lesson, Pinocchio learned the hard way that the road to becoming "a real boy" requires that he complete all of the steps; in other words, there are no shortcuts. Remember the first day when he set out for school so he could learn how to be "a real boy"? On the way, he ran into "Honest" John the Fox. Upon learning about the little puppet's intentions, "Honest" John saw an excellent opportunity to take advantage of his inexperienced friend and suggested there was a shortcut to success—become an actor! In other words, he suggested, "Fake it 'til you make it."

What happened next was a real eye opener for Pinocchio, who soon realized that instead of becoming "a real boy," he now had even more external strings attached because he was in bondage and being exploited by Stromboli. It's painful to admit our mistakes, but it is obvious that shortcuts don't get us where we want to go. Becoming "a real boy" is just that: *becoming*. **There are no tricks or shortcuts**. Each step is critical if you are going to be "real"!

Activity 19

There Are No Financial Shortcuts

Use this activity to identify financial shortcuts that may sound appealing but will actually limit your freedom instead.

1. What financial shortcuts has this book warned about in previous chapters?

2. What financial shortcuts have you taken or seen others take? What were the consequences?

3. If there truly are no shortcuts, what is the only way to achieve financial freedom?

CHAPTER TWENTY

Lesson Number Two:

NOTHING IS FREE.

A fter the disappointing attempt at shortcuts, Pinocchio determined to go back to school. Just as you might guess, "Honest" John reappears on the scene to console Pinocchio and manipulatively suggest that he'd been taken advantage of and that he was now an official member of the victim's club. What Pinocchio deserved now, suggested "Honest" John, was a trip to Pleasure Island. On Pleasure Island, Pinocchio could do anything he wanted and never have any consequences, and best of all, on Pleasure Island, everything is free.

So, trusting "Honest" John, Pinocchio boarded the boat to a life of carefree indulgence. At first, it was great. No supervision, no hours, all the food, candy, alcohol, and tobacco he could consume. What could be better? Except the longer they stayed on the island, he and the other boys began to grow tails, snouts, and hoofs. That's right. They were turning into dumb animals. The more they indulged, the dumber they became.

Once their transformation was complete, the lazy, self-indulgent boys were crated up and shipped off to work in the salt mines. Being doomed to a future life of hard labor and no opportunity, Pinocchio soon recognized, this was not freedom. Once again, his actions added external strings instead of removing them. This time, he learned that **you cannot indulge without consequence**, and in fact, **nothing is free**.

After a narrow escape and a valuable lesson learned, Pinocchio decided it was time to return home, make things right with his father, and get back on the path to becoming "a real boy." There is nothing like learning for yourself—unless you are smart enough to learn from others.

Activity 20
Indulgence on "Pleasure Island" Has a Price
Identify indulgence and avoid the negative consequences.
1. What indulgences have you made or seen others make that have limited their financial freedom?
2. What was the price, or consequence, of these indulgences?
3. What is the only way to remove external strings of control and achieve freedom?

CHAPTER TWENTY-ONE

Lesson Number Three:

EVERYONE MUST FACE MONSTRO.

Upon returning home, Pinocchio discovered that his father had gone searching for his lost puppet and through a series of misfortunes ended up being swallowed by Monstro, the whale. Without much hope of escape, Geppetto resigned himself to spending the rest of his days imprisoned in the whale's belly.

Here was Pinocchio's big chance to redeem himself and show that he was brave and unselfish. Determined to rescue his father, he set out for the ocean floor in search of the biggest obstacle he had ever faced, Monstro. Through creativity, perseverance, and a great deal of personal risk, he managed to get the giant whale to open his mouth and allow his victim to flee captivity and race to safety.

The ensuing escape and subsequent chase actually cost Pinocchio his life. The surprise is that in losing his life, he actually gained it. In his case, it was the act of offering the ultimate sacrifice that proved beyond any doubt that he was brave, truthful, and unselfish. In doing so, he again earned the attention of the Blue Fairy who had given him the ability to be animated in the first place. This time, she returned to bestow upon him the gift of life and becoming "real."

Isn't that how it goes for the rest of us as well? Just like Pinocchio, we have to learn the lessons of life. The sooner we figure out that there are no shortcuts, that nothing is free of consequence, and that we must face intimidating obstacles, the sooner we achieve the desire of our hearts. And the only way to do it is to be brave, truthful, and unselfish. As we do so, not only do we become more "real," but others around us become more "real" to us as well. We begin to see their wants and needs in the same light that we see our own. Just like Pinocchio, we will find that **the best way to solve our own problems and achieve our own goals is to help others solve their problems and achieve their goals**.

Becoming "a real boy," financially speaking, is no different. There are laws that govern the outcomes we desire. Therefore, it behooves us to learn the requirements of those laws and do them. For most of us, this is not an easy process. We must change the way we think and act if we really want to enjoy financial freedom. Doing the right thing in the right way and at the right time will require **discipline**, or in other words, **honesty**, **bravery**, and **unselfishness**.

Activity 21

Gaining Discipline and Freedom

Displaying honesty, bravery, and unselfishness in all aspects of our lives, including finances, will yield discipline and ultimately, freedom.

1. What obstacles, or fears, hold you back from financial freedom? How do you plan to overcome those fears?

2. Once you overcome your fears, how do you plan to help others?

CHAPTER TWENTY-TWO

BECOME "A REAL BOY" BY BUILDING A SOLID FINANCIAL PLAN

S o, you want to become "a real boy" and be financially free? Let's take a look at what will be required of you. You've already learned most of the key elements so far. Now, let's put them together and build a solid financial plan.

Building a solid financial plan is a step-by-step process, and each phase must be done in order.[5] Of course, if you have lots of financial resources, you can complete all of these phases simultaneously, but there

---

5   To create your one-page annual financial plan and for other helpful tools for implementing the above five steps, go to www.resetyourbarcode.com. This fee-based, lifetime membership website will guide you through the financial planning process and make planning easy and effective.

is still an order when it comes to your priorities. Here are the five phases to building a financial plan.

1. Controlled Spending.
2. Protection.
3. Emergency and Opportunity Savings.
4. Debt Reduction.
5. Growing Your Money.

Phase One: Controlled Spending

Controlled spending doesn't mean that you have to be on an austere budget that inflicts pain and never allows you to have any fun, but it does mean that **you should know where every penny goes and make sure that the spending supports your other financial goals**. Controlled spending means deciding in advance what you're going to spend money on, and when the money is spent, you stop spending.

Phase One is the first priority. To complete Phase One, you must establish a budget that incorporates saving as well as spending. A budget is simply a matter of comparing what is coming in to what is going out and then making adjustments to the outgoing so that there is something left over to save. I recommend that you **save 20% of your net income**.

Phase Two: Protection

Protection is **the money that shows up when needed most**. It is the dollars that you purchased with pennies as you bought life insurance, disability insurance, health insurance, auto and home insurance, and so on. Having the right amount and the right kind of protection in place allows you the freedom to go out into the world and do what you do, knowing that money will show up even when you can't.

Phase Two is your next priority. To complete Phase Two, you must add up all of your life insurance benefits. Add up all of your debt and subtract it from the life insurance benefits. Next, calculate what kind of monthly income the difference will provide. If there is not enough money to support your survivors, buy more life insurance. I recommend you **leave your dependents debt free and with enough income that they can continue to live the lifestyle you were planning to live together**.

Phase Three: Emergency and Opportunity Savings

Once you've completed Phase One and Phase Two, you're ready to complete Phase Three by building Emergency and Opportunity Savings. This is the **short-term liquid money** available to cover short periods of unemployment, the deductible on a policy, or small emergencies that are better off being paid from savings rather than insurance. Once the emergency portion is in place, keep saving and grow some opportunity money. This is money that can be used to reduce debt or take advantage of excellent investment opportunities.

Phase Four: Debt Reduction

One of the best investments you will ever make is paying off debt. When debt is paid off, you have a guaranteed return of the interest you will no longer be required to pay. Plus, you will have the peace of mind that comes from knowing that even if income drops off or goes away, you will not have to face the collectors who come to take what you thought was yours. You know, debt does not disappear just because income does. **When you are debt free, you are in charge of how much you want to earn, how long you want to work, and what you want to do with your time**. Otherwise, someone else will always be making that decision for you.

When the first three Phases are complete, you're ready to move on to Phase Four. To complete Phase Four, begin paying off debt. List all your debts in order, starting with the worst. Then, while still making payments on the other debts, begin paying off the worst debt. When that debt is paid off, take the money you were using to pay it off and "double down," or increase the payment on the next debt. Continue this process until all your debts are paid.

Phase Five: Growing Your Money

Growing your money is about two things. First, growing money is **systematically setting some money aside** so it can accumulate and earn interest or appreciate in an appropriate investment. This way, it grows not only in amount but in its ability to provide independence and dignity in your old age. Second, growing money is **putting your money in the right place in the first place**. These days, where you have your money is as important as how much money you have, because if it is in the wrong place, much—or even all—of it could evaporate right before your eyes.

Congratulations! You've reached the final phase of building a solid financial plan. Now that you have controlled spending, protection in place, emergency and opportunity savings, and eliminated debt, you can move on to Phase Five. To learn more about completing Phase Five, see Chapter Twenty-Three.

The above five phases are your guide to achieving financial freedom. Move through and complete them in order, setting goals annually, in order to reach your objective of becoming "a real boy," financially speaking, *with no strings attached.*

Activity 22

A One-Page Annual Financial Plan

Achieve freedom through planning. Your annual financial plan starts when you answer these questions.

1. Do you have a spending plan?
2. How does it help you accomplish your financial goals?
3. When was the last time you evaluated your protection for life insurance, etc.? Is it up to date?
4. How much is currently in your emergency fund?
5. How much should be in your emergency fund, and how long until you will have it?
6. How much debt do you currently have?
7. Is that debt really necessary?
8. What is your plan to eliminate your debt?
9. Where do you have your long-term growth money, and is it properly classified?
10. How much money will you need in the future in order for you to be independent and live without external strings attached?

CHAPTER TWENTY-THREE

PHASE FIVE:
GROWING YOUR MONEY

P hase Five in building a solid financial plan is growing your money. Remember, you should choose carefully where to put your money to ensure its safety. Be sure to put it in the right place in the first place.

What Is Asset Classification?

So how do you know where to put your money so it will be there when you need it? You classify your assets before you do diversification and allocation. So what is asset classification? It's a simple process of classifying your money into one or more of the three following classifications: **investor money**, **accumulator money**, or **gambler money**.

What Is Investor Money?

In order to be classified as investor money, it must meet the following qualifications. As noted in Chapter Eight, **it must be "walk away money."** This means that you must be able to walk away from this money emotionally as well as financially without it endangering your financial security and freedom. In other words, it has to be money that you will not need in the future. Real investors never speculate with money they cannot afford to lose.

If you have "walk away money," you can't consider yourself an investor just yet. There are two more aspects to investing. First, **you must possess specialized knowledge** about any investment you might put your money in. Real investors never invest in anything they don't understand well. Second, **you must be in a position to influence the outcome of your investment**. Though you cannot *control* the outcome, you must be able to *influence* it. Real investors never leave things up to chance. They must have the ability to use their specialized knowledge to improve the odds of a favorable outcome.

Just for the record, I do make one exception to the "walk away" rule. Namely, if you are investing in your own business to provide your income, you are the exception—so long as you have the ability to use your specialized knowledge to influence how your investment, or business, performs. When you have "walk away money," specialized knowledge, and influence, you deserve the potential that comes with being an investor.

What Is Accumulator Money?

The second classification is accumulator money. The qualification for accumulator money is pretty simple. First, **you cannot afford to lose this money**. You will need it at some point in the future. Your retirement funds are a good representation of money you will need later on. Accumulator money is the kind of money that *must* be there when you need it. Not maybe, not probably, but *definitely*.

Second, if **you don't really understand an investment prospect**, you're probably not in a position to consider yourself an investor. You may simply not know how an investment works or have the time or interest to take proper care of it. In other words, you don't have the specialized knowledge to do it yourself.

Third, you are probably dealing with accumulator money if **you are not in a position to influence the outcome**. In other words, you either don't know what to do or you own such a small portion that you have no say in how the investment is being managed.

When these three qualifications are in place, you don't have investor money; you have accumulator money. **Instead of** *potential,* **you need to have** *guarantees*. You need to know that your principal is protected and that your money will grow. This is the only way to know what you will have and when you will have it. When I say guarantees, I mean the kind you get from the banks, credit unions, and insurance companies. Keep in mind that not all guarantees are created equal, so check out the safety ratings and make sure that your institution has the ability to make good on its promises.

What Is Gambler Money?

The third classification is gambler money. You see, when you gamble, **you are putting money at risk that you cannot afford to walk away from**. You don't understand the risk and have no way to mitigate it. Since you don't have guarantees, **you must depend on luck**. When luck determines the outcome, you are gambling. Now please don't get me wrong. I'm not saying that you can't or shouldn't gamble; that is entirely up to you. I am simply stating that when you can't afford to lose the money, don't know what you're doing, and have no way to influence the outcome, you are gambling.

To Beat Investment Risk, Should I Diversify?

We have been taught for years that the best way to beat financial risk is to diversify and to asset allocate. I think it is important to put this process into proper perspective. The purpose of **asset allocation** is to create what is called the "efficient frontier," or simply **trying to achieve maximum growth potential with the least amount of risk**. This is best accomplished by choosing investments from various asset classes that are negatively correlated. This way when one asset class is falling, another may be rising. While this helps to soften the impact of loss, it also waters down the potential for gain.

But asset allocation is irrelevant if your money shouldn't be at risk in the first place. The important thing to understand is if you are planning asset allocation, you should be using "investor money," money you can afford to lose. If you cannot afford to lose the money, it should not be put at risk. Further, you should only invest in things you understand and be in a position to exercise influence over the outcome.

How Can I Beat Inflation?

We have also been taught that if we are not taking risk, we will not be able to keep up with inflation. While I agree that keeping up with inflation is challenging, I would like to emphasize the fact that **you do not beat inflation with speculation**, or gambling; rather, **you beat inflation with accumulation**. How do you beat inflation when you are losing principal because of risk that you have no control over? Again, the only time you should put your money at risk is when you know what you are doing and have the ability to influence the outcome. Even then, it should be money that you can live without. Otherwise, it belongs in guaranteed accounts.

Asset Classification Is the First Step

So, **before you try to decide how to diversify and allocate your growth money, be sure to classify it**. Make sure you know what kind of money you have. Also, be sure that you can live with the investment results so you aren't disappointed and find yourself in need of money that isn't available. This way, you will put it in the right place in the first place. Remember, *where* your money is at is as important as *how much* money you have.

Finally, with any part of financial management, remember you can only control three things:

1. The number of years you work.
2. The number of dollars you save.
3. The places you put your money.

With correct asset classification, you can ensure you put your money in the right place, exercising control over your financial future. As you plan your future finances so that you can finance your future plans, keep in mind that if you are planning on things you cannot control, you may actually be putting together a "financial hope" rather than a financial plan.

Activity 23

Begin Asset Classification

Know how much money you will need in the future, and then classify your money so you can be sure you've put it in the right place.

1. How many years do you plan to continue working?
2. How much money are you going to save this year?
3. Review where you are growing your money. Have you classified your money correctly?

MAKING THREE IMPORTANT CHOICES ON YOUR FINANCIAL JOURNEY

In this section, you'll learn how to complete the fourth step in resetting your financial barcode, Step 4—"The G.P.S. Experience." This step is important because it advises you how to handle detours and avoid pitfalls that can derail you in your journey toward financial freedom. This section also offers practical advice that will help you move forward with the solid financial plan you have developed.

In "The G.P.S. Experience," you will come to understand the importance of always knowing **where you are relative to where you want to go** and the **best way to get there**. The following choices will help you chart a good course and be able to stick with it. The three choices you must make are

1. **Select good advisors.**
2. **Choose good products.**
3. **Practice accountability.**

THE FOURTH STEP,
OR "THE G.P.S. EXPERIENCE"

G.P.S. stands for Global Positioning
System. Most modern cars and phones
have a G.P.S., or navigating system,
that helps travelers arrive at their
desired destinations. Let's take a look
at the process. First, you determine
your desired destination and its global location, usually an address or
coordinates. Once you've entered the information indicating where you
want to go, the G.P.S. sends a signal to triangulate your information
between satellites and sends it back to you. In the process, it can tell
you where you are, where you want to go, and the best way to get there.

Because there is a constant signal between your G.P.S. unit and the
satellites, you receive continual feedback so you always know where you
are relative to where you want to go. One of the great benefits of a G.P.S.
is that it prevents you from becoming lost and wasting valuable time.
Another awesome benefit provided by the G.P.S. is that when you get

off track because of road blocks, traffic jams, or detours, etc., the system doesn't call you out or tell you how stupid you are or that you will never reach your destination. It simply says, "Recalculating." It adjusts its suggested route, based on your new position. In essence, it says, "Now that you're here, this will be the best way to get you to your destination."

When you think about how a G.P.S. works, it is easy to see how it relates to your financial planning and well-being. Having financial goals and a good financial plan that you review and reset each year works in a similar way. First, deciding where you want to go and then taking stock of where you are currently helps you chart an efficient course toward your "desired destination," or financial goals. Keeping your goals continually in front of you gives you constant feedback or reminders of what you are trying to accomplish.

Because life is what it is, there will be road blocks, traffic jams, detours, and other obstacles that will come up and try to derail you from reaching your goals. When the obstacles come, remember what the G.P.S. does: it says, "Recalculating." It asks, "Now that I'm here, what is the best way to get to my destination?" By doing annual accounting and course correcting, any detours will be short-lived, time wasted will be kept to a minimum, and you will back on your way to the financial destination of your choice.

CHAPTER TWENTY-FOUR

First Choice:

SELECT GOOD ADVISORS.

T he first choice you'll make in "The G.P.S. Experience" is selecting a financial advisor. Not all advisors are created equal. I've seen people get detoured and lose valuable time in accomplishing their financial goals because they took advice from the wrong person.

Why do you need a financial advisor? Once you have a plan, you will likely need to purchase financial tools in order to implement it. Many financial tools must be purchased through a licensed advisor. Plus, a good advisor can help you choose the tools that will best support your objectives. So how do you choose a good advisor? Try evaluating a prospective advisor based on these 10 qualities.

Personality

Before you hire a financial advisor, do a quick personality check. Make sure you like and trust the advisor you're considering. Sometimes there is that little voice somewhere in the back of your mind telling you something isn't right. When that happens, be sure to listen. There is usually a good reason it's speaking to you. Remember, if something sounds too good to be true, it probably is.

Education

A financial advisor with a solid education is key. Don't just look for college degrees. Pay attention to how much industry-specific education your prospective advisor has taken during her career. What credentials has she earned? In other words, is she staying current?

Experience

Next, look at experience. Not only should you note how many years a financial advisor has been in his career, but also, how much experience has he had during those years? Some have twenty years of experience, while others have one year of experience twenty times. The difference is worth noting. If you consider a financial advisor with limited experience, evaluate his potential. Does he have back-up support? Is he committed to learning and growing with you through the years?

Associations

Your financial advisor's community should also be a factor in your decision. Make sure you know who she associates with professionally. Examine not just company affiliations, but also note which professional associations she belongs to. Does she actively participate and contribute to these affiliations?

Specialty

Just like you would choose a doctor based on his area of expertise know what specialized knowledge or skills your potential financial advisor possesses. What is his primary focus, and where does at least 60-70% of his income come from? No one is good at everything. Find out what his specialty is, and then decide if it's a service you want or need.

References

Know whether others would recommend this advisor. Will your potential advisor give you at least 5 references? After contacting these references, consider, what did you learn from those references about her personality, education, experience, ongoing service, and specialty? You might ask the references the same questions that you ask the advisor and compare answers.

Principles

By reading this book, you have learned some important financial principles. Will your potential financial advisor adhere to financial principles? Are his principles consistent with the principles discussed in this book? Will he make sure that all product and planning recommendations support your plan?

Example

You can tell a lot about a person's financial priorities by examining how they live. Is your financial advisor living correct financial principles? How do you know? Is she willing to share her own financial plan? Remember, you can learn a lot about a person when you see what she does with her own money.

Accountability

A relationship with a financial advisor is just that—an ongoing relationship. Choose an advisor who plans to develop a working relationship over many years. Ask, will he commit to an annual meeting to review results and forecast into the future? Is he willing to assist in resetting your plan each year?

Compensation

Of course, you're hiring a professional, so make sure you know the cost beforehand. How will you compensate your financial advisor? What does she charge for initial consultation and plan design? And what is the cost of ongoing service? Remember, there are only 100 pennies in a dollar.

Selecting the right advisor will keep you on track toward your future financial destination. Be sure to carefully evaluate and consider these 10 factors to be sure you've chosen the right advisor, one that you can depend on for years to come.

Activity 24

Choose a Good Advisor

Evaluating your current or potential financial advisor will ensure you receive sound advice based on financial principles.

1. How did you choose your current advisor, or how do you plan to go about choosing your financial advisor?
2. What questions will you ask your advisor to be sure the relationship is a "good fit"?
3. What evidence will you look for to evaluate whether you will receive sound advice based on financial principles?

CHAPTER TWENTY-FIVE

Second Choice:

CHOOSE GOOD PRODUCTS.

T he next choice you will face during "The G.P.S. Experience" concerns financial products, such as life insurance, annuities, banking instruments, and investments. Although your financial advisor may recommend products, it's important that you know some basic features of financial products since not all products are created equal. The following seven points may be useful in comparing and selecting the products best suited to your purposes.

Safety

First and foremost, don't gamble with your retirement money. Choose safe, **low-risk products**. Compare product guarantees and the financial safety ratings of the institutions behind them. Check out multiple rating services and make sure you understand how the guarantees work. Your financial advisor can assist you.

Accessibility

How accessible is your money? How much access do you need? Next to safety, one of the most important things is **the ability to get your money when you need it**. However, if you have too much access to that money, it might make it too easy to spend. Careless spending may reduce the amount of potential earnings. Decide how much you need immediately accessible, and then put the rest to work in the right place.

Return

Rate of return, or the **earning potential** of a financial product, is an important consideration, but it should never be placed before safety and access. Once the required levels of safety and access are met, you are free to pursue the best possible rate of return.

Taxation

Never make a financial decision based solely on tax issues. Having said that, you should never make a financial or investment decision without considering the tax implications. Believe it or not, we have two sets of tax laws, one for the informed and one for the uninformed. The uninformed run the very high risk of paying more than they should. However, the informed know **there is no moral obligation to pay more than the law requires**. Once issues like safety, accessibility, and rate of return have been considered, look for the best possible outcome relative to taxes.

Income

What is the possibility that you will need to derive regular income from your money during the period it will be in the product you are considering? If there is a reasonable chance that you might, be sure the product you are considering has options for making income available without causing you to pay a penalty. If you are definitely planning on taking income from this product, **be sure it is built to provide income**. Compare the different income options and choose the one that is right for you.

Cost

By now, you should know that nothing is free. However, a careful analysis of the costs involved with the available product choices will help you to get the best possible value. Everything has a cost. **Some costs are very justifiable, and some are unnecessary**. Be sure to understand all of the charges involved, and you will be able to make a regret-free selection. Still, never let cost alone be the determining factor. Keep safety, access, return, and taxes in mind when you consider the cost.

Death or Illness

The way an investment or product is owned can have a big influence on what happens when you die or require extended medical care. Some forms of ownership require probate, and others do not. Be sure you know how your money will be disbursed when the unexpected happens. For example, life insurance and annuities pay proceeds directly to beneficiaries and do not require probate. A little research can ensure your plan will operate the way you want it to.

The financial products you choose are as important as the amount of money you have. Use these seven points, and you will gain clarity and understanding. The more you know, the more you improve the quality of your selection.

Activity 25

Choose Good Financial Products

Evaluate the financial products you own or are considering purchasing.

1. What product are you considering?
2. How safe will your money be? Will you be able to access the money, if needed?
3. What rate of return do you expect from this product? Have you considered the tax benefits?
4. Will the product provide income? Are there hidden costs?
5. How will the product pay out in case of death or illness?

CHAPTER TWENTY-SIX

Third Choice:

PRACTICE ACCOUNTABILITY.

A nother important part of "The G.P.S. Experience" is learning to be accountable—in other words, doing **regular financial check-ups**. Think of it as your money's annual physical exam. Like a visit to the doctor, some people view accountability as something to be avoided. They are afraid that it will make them do something they don't want to do. The simple fact is that accountability actually helps you do what you want most: it keeps you on the path you've chosen by telling you how you are doing along the way. Since there will always be more to do than you can possibly ever get done, it is critical to chart your course and then have a system for holding yourself accountable so you can make regular course corrections as needed.

Most important of all, accountability makes it possible to recognize and celebrate your progress. Without the ability to measure and celebrate your progress, you would soon get off track and lose your way. When this happens, your goals go by the wayside and progress stops.

Schedule a Financial Check-Up

To maintain your financial accountability, just follow the nine steps below.

1. First, access a copy of your current annual financial plan.
2. Next, input your current asset information into the plan to take an accounting of your current asset growth.
3. Schedule an accountability session with your advisors. Occasionally meeting with all of them together helps them be accountable in front of their professional peers.
4. Share your plan and current financial results with your advisors.
5. Together with your advisors, measure your progress and make any course corrections that are necessary.
6. Celebrate your success. It's always a good idea to acknowledge when things are going well.
7. Then, if necessary, update and revise your plan. Set your financial priorities and number them in order of importance. Remember not to plan too many tasks, or you might become overwhelmed and not do any.
8. Set the date for your next accountability session now. There is extreme power in setting deadlines and sticking to them.
9. Repeat the process. Do it every year until you reach your financial goals and have more money than you know what to do with, and then do it again!

Accountability is your friend. It will help you get what you want and allow you to enjoy the process.

Making wise, well-informed choices is the next step to gaining financial freedom. Be sure to select good advisors, choose appropriate financial products, and schedule frequent accountability sessions. These three choices are your own financial G.P.S. With them, you'll know **where you are**, **where you want to go**, and **how you are going to get there**.

Activity 26
Schedule an Accountability Session

Checking in with your financial advisors and reviewing your plan annually will keep you on the path to financial freedom.

1. When was the last time you held a meeting with all of your advisors to review your annual financial plan? If it was more than a year ago, schedule a date now.
2. Prepare for the meeting by evaluating your annual plan and current asset growth.
3. With your advisors, decide. What changes should you make to your annual financial plan to keep you on track?
4. What action will you take following the meeting?
5. Finally, schedule the date of your next accountability session.

USE YOUR NEWFOUND FINANCIAL FREEDOM TO GIVE BACK

In this section, you'll learn how to complete the final step in resetting your financial barcode, Step 5—"The Johnny Appleseed Experience." This step takes you beyond your journey to freedom, helping you live the future that will be yours once you achieve your goals.

Consider everything you've accomplished by following the first four steps to reset your financial barcode. You understand financial principles. You have a solid financial plan in place. You are resetting it every year and watching your financial dreams become reality. So, what do you do next? "The Johnny Appleseed Experience" answers this question.

Many people feel that the secret to happiness and success is to get the most out of life, but I believe real happiness and real success is more about having life get the most out of you! The way to have life get the most out of you is for *you* to put the *most* into life.

THE FIFTH STEP, OR "THE JOHNNY APPLESEED EXPERIENCE"

I love the story of John Chapman, better known as Johnny Appleseed. John lived from 1774 to 1845. His life became a legend because of his interest in apples and his great contribution to the settlers who were migrating West during this period. Because of his love of God, people, and apples,  Johnny Appleseed traveled ahead of many of the settlers and planted apple orchards which helped to provide food to the migrating throngs who were pushing the country farther and farther West.

John understood the "pay it forward" concept and truly lived it. When you are the beneficiary of a good deed, the "pay it forward" principle instructs that you "repay" the benefactor by doing a good deed for someone else, in essence, "paying" the good deed "forward" for others.

Johnny Appleseed's story is a living illustration of the saying, "You can count the seeds in an apple, but you can't count the apples in a seed." His mission in life was to always leave things better than he found them and to prepare the way for others who would come after him. His service and concern for others earned him a place in history as a legendary hero. In contrast to another great legend of American folklore, Johnny Appleseed was not known for his ability to quickly cut down trees but rather for his ability to grow them.

Everywhere he went, Johnny Appleseed planted and cultivated orchards of beautiful, life-sustaining apple trees. His trees produced apples, the apples produced seeds, and the seeds in turn produced more trees.

When a person lives his life in such a way that he is always planting "seeds," or "paying it forward," he will find—at a most unexpected time—that he may feast upon the very fruit that came from seeds he planted long ago. We've all heard the expression that "what goes around comes around." Not only is this saying very true, but it is a very good reason for each of us to do all in our power to give our best efforts daily and plant "seeds" at every opportunity. Who knows? It may just be you who enjoys the fruit of your labor most of all.

CHAPTER TWENTY-SEVEN

WHAT WE LEARN
FROM JOHNNY APPLESEED

T he life of Johnny Appleseed teaches us an important lesson: *plant seeds*. So, what is planting seeds? Simply put, **planting seeds is reaching out with your resources, time, and talents to ease a burden, spread happiness, and improve the quality of someone's life**. Planting seeds is an obligation that falls upon each of us. Think about it. We all drink from wells we didn't dig!

You can't say to yourself, "That's not for me." For, whether you know it or not, you plant seeds every day that change the world, which in turn will change *your* world. Make your contribution one that will change things for the better.

Just imagine a world where everyone is working to make things better for those who will follow after them. When one person does something good and nice for just three people who in turn do an act of service or kindness for three more, one becomes three, three becomes nine, nine becomes twenty-seven, and in just twenty layers of giving, doing, and "paying it forward," more than one billion people would be touched. But don't wait for it to come to you; be a starter today.

How Do I Plant Seeds?

When do you plant seeds? Now! Start today. Everyone can do something for someone, even if that someone hasn't been born yet.

Where do you plant seeds? Where are you now? That's a good place to begin. On your journey to financial success, you will be placed in circumstances that will create the perfect opportunity for you to use your time, talents, and money to make a positive difference.

How do you plant seeds? Start by putting more into life by giving more of yourself to it. This is best done by doing the little things that show your love and respect for others, especially those closest to you. Kind words, kind deeds, anonymous acts of service, and supporting good causes are all ways to make someone else's life a little better.

Why do you plant seeds? The fact is, you plant seeds every day, whether you are trying to or not. The question is, what kind of seeds are they? Someday, you will live in the world you are creating today. Wouldn't you want to make it a great place for everyone? Making the world a great place for others will make it a great place for you!

Be a starter. Don't just share apples; plant apple trees, and keep it going. If all of us do our part, we never have to worry about running out of apple goodness.

Always remember, **the way to get the most out of life is to have *life* get the most out of *you*.** Do this by putting the *most* of *you* into life.

Activity 27

How Are You Giving Back?

Consider what seeds you are planting right now and what seeds you will plant in the future.

1. Look around you right now. How could you use your time, talents, and financial resources to touch one person's life in a positive and unexpected way?
2. How could you create a daily habit of finding one good deed or act of service to do for someone else?
3. What is a good cause that you are passionate about? What is one thing you could do today to support it?
4. Name three things that someone else has done for you that have made your life better.

A FINAL WORD

Doing a financial reset is a perfect way to reset your barcode and improve the value of your contribution to your own life, as well as to others. A financial reset is easy to do. Just follow the five steps described in this book, and you will find that your money can work for you instead of you always working for it.

Five Steps to Reset Your Financial Barcode

1. **"The Glass Slipper Experience."** Learn the principles that govern the results you want to achieve, and do what they require of you. Become the perfect fit for what you want to receive.

2. **"The Ebenezer Experience."** Give yourself a regular wakeup call and make sure that your financial values are compatible with correct financial principles. Try using the Wants vs. Needs Test to make sure you will be pleased with your purchases. Track

your spending so you can control what you are spending where. Lastly, be sure to regularly forecast your present efforts into the future to see if you will be pleased with the results.

3. **"The Wooden Puppet Experience**." Become "a real boy," financially speaking. Put together a financial plan and use it to remove financial strings, or outside controls, so you can be financially free.

4. **"The G.P.S. Experience**." A financial plan does little good if you do not review it often and make adjustments as your circumstances change. Accountability and course correction are what keep you on track.

5. **"The Johnny Appleseed Experience**." Having all the money in the world doesn't mean much if you have no one to share it with. Money does its best work when it is used to make the world a better place. Taking charge of your finances will empower you to do more, give more, and enjoy the process more. Remember: you can count the seeds in an apple, but you can't count the apples in a seed.

One of the most important freedoms we enjoy is economic freedom. Religious freedom, social freedom, and political freedom rest on the foundation of economic freedom. When you give up economic freedom, the others will soon follow. A nation is no stronger than its citizens. If we want to remain a free people and a strong nation, we must return to the sound principles of individual economic freedom.

When you are strong, you can help others be strong. When we are strong together, we preserve all of our freedoms and remain a strong nation. A strong nation can have a huge influence for good in the world. Always remember: when you change *your* world, you change *the* world! It's up to you!

If you are serious about financial freedom, we can help. Visit our website at www.resetyourbarcode.com. Your one-time fee will provide unlimited lifetime access to financial resources that will set you on the path to economic freedom and creating a better world for you and those around you. See you there.

NOTE TO READERS

ABOUT THE AUTHOR

Marvin R. Reynolds is the founder of Reset YOUR Barcode Training Academy, a training / consulting company that helps financial advisors, individuals, and organizations achieve breakthrough performance with breakthrough preparation. As a trainer and speaker, Marv draws upon his many years of sales, management, and leadership experience to help people across the country implement his unique 5-step process to break through personal barriers and achieve financial success.

Marv knows that great potential is a heavy burden until you master the 5 steps of resetting your barcode and turn your potential into power.

Having overcome overwhelming adversity himself, Marv understands the challenges and misinformation that many people deal with. Through personal experience and observation, Marv has identified the core principles for developing the character and competence needed to achieve real wealth and happiness.

Experience:

- Public speaking at industry and non-industry events and universities.
- Personal performance coaching for individuals and businesses.
- Agency management and personal production as a financial advisor.
- Co-founder of Tribo-luminescence, a personal and leadership development company.
- Earned many prestigious awards for agency management, manpower development, and personal production in the financial services industry.
- Graduate of the Leadership in Life Institute.
- Served in many leadership positions in community and industry.

Designations:

- Chartered Financial Consultant and Life Underwriter Training Council Fellow (through the American College at Bryn Mar, Pennsylvania).

Meet Marv online and receive free training at www.resetyourbarcode.com.